AUSTRALIAN PARAKEETS

AND THEIR MUTATIONS

HERMAN KREMER

ISBN 90-73217-03-2

Front cover   : Rock Pebbler Parakeet

Photography : Cees Scholtz

Illustrations : Bauke Vliegendehond

Published by: Uitgeverij 'Ornis'
de Zwette 58
NL-9257 RR NOORDBERGUM
the Netherlands
tel. 05110 - 3589
fax 05110 - 3549

CONTENTS

I. Introduction

The keeping and breeding of parakeets and parrots has gone through a period of rapid development during the last twenty years. In the seventies and at the beginning of the eighties especially, many species became available to the fancier.

During the seventies in particular thousands of enthusiasts in Britain and in western Europe took up this hobby as a way of filling their free time. Partly due to this massive boom, breeding successes were achieved with numerous species, and as a result people with a lighter purse were able to afford the majority of them. The increasing amount of leisure time and the rise in incomes also played an important role.

When about 1960 Australia banned the export of flora and fauna the fanciers were suddenly dependent on the stock of birds already in captivity. As a result it became more necessary than it had been to devote attention to breeding; after all, losses could no longer be replaced by the import of shipments of new parakeets. In a number of cases at first it was only with the greatest difficulty that certain species could be encouraged to breed successfully. Birds which now almost have to be restrained in their urge to breed were then problem cases, the Splendid Parakeet is a case in point. Over the years, however, we have gained a wealth of experience and we are able to achieve breeding success with most species of Australian parakeets in captivity here. This has, among other things, meant that these birds have retained their great appeal. They have a number of qualities which set them apart from other members of the parakeet and parrot family; they are brightly coloured, it is often easy to tell the cock and the hen apart, they do not scream but produce a pleasant sound, they are not destructive, and they are fairly easy to care for and breed.

A disadvantage is that they do not become attached to their keepers like the South American species do. Australian parakeets are more loners; in the aviary they will always keep some distance between themselves and their mate.

With the growth of the hobby more literature appeared on the market; not only magazines but also books in various languages.

A number of times during contact with several aviculturists the need for a concise, clear, informative, and practical book about all the species of Australian parakeets found in our aviaries was apparent. After some thought I decided to make an attempt to fill this need. The result is the book here before you. The accent has been placed on practical information, which means that this book is not so much aimed at the very experienced aviculturist as at the person who is yet to become one. The information is given by means of text and pictures; a photo of every species showing the appearance and, where relevant, the difference between the sexes of the bird concerned is therefore included. Experience has taught us that a photo has much more appeal and is clearer than a description of the plumage of a bird. The differences between the various species are also shown to their best advantage.

Besides these there are also a number of photos of mutations included. Although that section does not form the main subject matter of this book, more and more are appearing and they can look forward to the attention of a growing number of aviculturists. Mutations deserve a place therefore, although they appeal to some more than to others. With regard to the various colour variations I am conscious of the fact that this book can only show the situation as it is now; new ones could even appear in the period between its writing and its publication. The developments will go on.

Almost all the photos were made specially for this book by Cees Scholtz. I am extremely grateful to him for the days that he spent travelling with me throughout the country in order to achieve the result you see here. This is also the place for a word of thanks to the aviculturists who freely made their birds available, and also to Bauke Vliegendehond who supplied the illustrations.

II. The country of origin: Australia

Although rumours had been circulating for centuries regarding a "Terra australis" or great "Southern Continent" that was supposed to lie to the south of Asia, it was not until 1606 that the Dutchman Willem Jansz, on a voyage of discovery to the south of Java in his ship "'t Duyfken", became the first European to sight the coast of North Australia. He mapped 200 miles of it.

With the increasing activities of the Europeans in that area the discovery of particularly Australia's west coast was bound to follow soon. In 1616 another Dutchman, Dirck Hartog, made the first recorded landing on Australian soil. The name that the country was given - New Holland - is still recalled in the scientific name of the Cockatiel: *Nymphicus hollandicus*.

During the course of the seventeenth century many captains belonging to the East India Company took part in the mapping of the coastline of this new continent. Abel Tasman for example made two great voyages in 1642-1643 and 1644 during which he discovered, among other things, the island which was later to be named Tasmania after him. Because the Australian inland seemed desolate and as no spices or precious metals were found, the Dutch did not lay any claim to this area.

However, they did not reach the east coast. There it was the English captain James Cook who in 1770 first set foot on land and claimed the country for England. This was at the spot where nowadays Sydney lies.

At first England did not see any value in this new continent either. And from 1787 onwards it was used for a long time only as a penal colony. Only in the middle of the nineteenth century did this come to an end and were free colonies established. These later became the states Western Australia, South Australia, Victoria, Queensland, New South Wales and the Northern Territory.

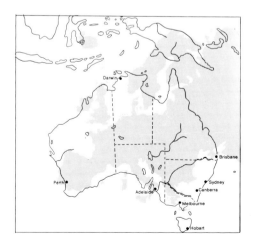

Australia and Europe are here drawn to the same scale over each other. This map gives a good impression of the relative sizes of the two continents

The Australian continent is about 25% smaller than Europe, and approximately the same size as the United States (excluding Alaska). It measures 2,500 miles from east to west and 2,000 miles from north to south. It has an area of 2,966,136 square miles and is therefore 31.5 times bigger than the United Kingdom, which has an area of 94,399 square miles. The coastline of Australia is 22,826 miles long and borders on three oceans and four seas. About 40% of the continent is tropical. It has a population of about fourteen million, which is about one quarter of that of the United Kingdom. In theory every Australian has got 126 times as much land available to him as every Briton. One way in which this manifests itself is in the manner in which houses are built. In the big cities such as Melbourne and Sydney nearly everyone lives in detached single family houses; there are as good as no high-rise buildings. This means that a lot of ground is necessary: a city such as Melbourne with little more than two million inhabitants covers an area about the size of Greater London!

Australia is the flattest of all the continents: less than half of it has an altitude of more than 500ft above sea level and a mere 5% rises to over 1,000ft. The only mountain range is on the east side: the Great Dividing Range, that runs north south. With its 7,310ft Mount Kosciusko is the highest point.

Another characteristic is the prevailing dryness. About 60% (mainly the extensive central area) has an annual rainfall of less than 10in (compared to Britain's 30in). Towards the coasts the rainfall gradually increases, even reaching 60in in the tropical north.

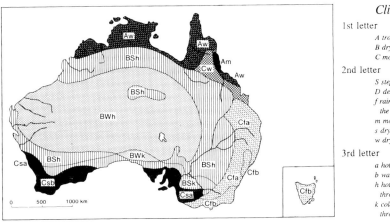

Climates

1st letter
A tropical rainforest
B dry climate
C moderate rainfall

2nd letter
S steppe climate
D desert climate
f rainfall throughout the year
m monsoon climate
s dry summer
w dry winter

3rd letter
a hot summer
b warm summer
h hot and dry throughout the year
k cold and dry throughout the year

The climate is for the most part subtropical, in the extreme north it is tropical and in the south more temperate. The following overview gives an impression of the average annual temperatures:

Sydney   17.1°C
Melbourne   13.7°C
Perth   18.1°C
Darwin   28.0°C
London   9.5°C

13

The distribution of the various forms of vegetation is strongly connected to the rainfall. A distinction can therefore be made between the different types, ranging from desert to tropical rainforest.

The central sand deserts are covered alternately with extensive growths of mulga (a type of acacia) and clumps of prickly spinifex grass. In a broad band in the south of this area, on the same soil sort, are found small multi-trunked eucalyptus trees alternating with low acacias and spinifex. Grassland containing solitary or groups of trees forms a wide band round the desert to the east and north. In the east the connection between the grassland and the coastal woodlands is formed by wooded savanna, a continuous parkland of trees and grass. The entire northern coastal area of the continent is covered with this type of vegetation. The real woods are limited to the coastal strips in the east and south; they are also found in the majority of Tasmania. Tropical rainforest is present only in small areas close by the sea in the east and north-east; these require high rainfall and a fertile soil.

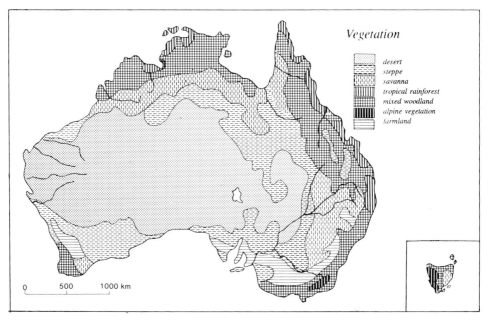

The maps showing climate and vegetation give more detailed information. In the individual descriptions in chapter IX the distribution of each species is given on a map. By comparing this with those on climate and vegetation one can see under which circumstances the species concerned lives in the wild. The aviculturist can possibly use that to his advantage.

Australia and the islands in the Pacific Ocean form one of the most clearly defined biological areas on earth. This is the result of a long history of isolation, because Australia has been cut off from other land masses by the sea for at least fifty million years. During this period life forms which were present in the continent or reached it later have been able to develop and evolve into all species imaginable: kangaroos, koalas, marsupial rats and wolves, lyre birds, cockatoos, parakeets, emus, gum trees (eucalyptuses), banksias, etc. etc.

Parakeets

Although, as mentioned earlier, the exploration of Australia or the unknown "Southern Continent" began in 1606 it was not until 1699 that the first member of the parakeet family (the Little Corella) was consciously recorded. The last (Marshall's Fig Parrot) was only discovered in 1947, 248 years later! The first parrotlike to reach Europe (England) alive was a Rainbow Lorikeet, and that was in 1789. The earliest known illustration is also of a Rainbow Lorikeet, published in 1774.

About a sixth of the total number of species of parrots and parakeets on earth occur in Australia. They are common in virtually all areas and in many parts of the country ten or more species can be found. The following overview gives a general picture of the ones that occur in this continent.

	species	subspecies
Lories and Lorikeets	6	1
Cockatoos	11	12
Fig Parrots	-	3
Red-cheeked Parrots	-	1
Eclectus Parrots	-	1
Ground Parakeet	1	1
Night Parakeet	1	-
other parakeets	29	19
	48	38

1. Countryside in southeastern Australia with bush-like eucalyptus trees or 'mallee'; in that part of the world the Barnard Parakeet is named after it: Mallee Ringneck Parakeet

In the remainder of this book only the last group, other parakeets, are dealt with; with one exception. All the species which are more or less common in our aviaries belong to this group. Three of them are not included: the Paradise Parakeet, the Rock Parakeet and the Orange-bellied Parakeet. These are not important as aviary birds.

That leaves, therefore, 26 species and 19 races from the Australian continent, plus the Cockatiel, which is usually classified as a cockatoo. Also included are a number of (sub)species which live on the islands round the continent, and show a relationship with the group mentioned and occur more or less frequently in aviaries. This applies to the Greenwinged King Parakeet, the Amboina King Parakeet, the Green Rosella, the Red-fronted Kakariki, the Yellow-fronted Kakariki and the Horned Parakeet.

2. *The Namoi River north of Sydney. In the trees that grow along it many (mostly Greater Sulphur-crested) Cockatoos spend the night*

3-4. Stephens Creek in the south-east of the country near Broken Hill. Here trees only grow along such-like water courses, which in summer are dry. These form a place of refuge for the parrot-likes present in the area, like the Little Corellas shown in the photo below, which it transpired were sitting in these same trees. They are often only visible once you have carefully explored the surroundings

17

III. Accomodation

Complete plan

Most aviculturists begin by building a couple of flights without realising what they are going to do in the future. This is inadvisable; many come to regret it. It is much much better to consider the total space available and to make one complete plan. That does not mean that it has to be carried out; it is no problem if you stop after five or ten aviaries. If you do want to carry on building it will prove only beneficial and convenient. For then you will have taken the following three points into account even before you start to build:
1.   the aviary must be suitable for the birds you want to keep;
2.   the aviary must be practical for you as aviculturist with regard to maintenance and care;
3.   the aviary must be as much as possible in keeping with the garden and house.

These preconditions already imply that most Australian parakeets are housed in aviaries built outside. Inside is also possible, but most aviculturists do not have the room there for large aviaries and the number of species that can be kept in cages is only limited. Besides, the favourable effects of the sun and rain on the birds' bodies and plumages are almost impossible to reproduce inside.
While making the complete plan you must take various matters into account. First and foremost is the positioning of the aviaries: are they to be placed facing north, east, south or west? Not every aviculturist has a free choice with regard to this, because the space available often imposes its own limitations, but if the choice is free the following advantages and disadvantages must be taken into account:
-      north facing: little sun, often cold wind and rain;
-      east facing: earlymorning sun, in the late afternoon none or less, in the summer warm dry wind, in the winter bitter cold wind, no rain driving in;
-      south facing: lots of sun from morning till night, variable   amounts of wind and rain blowing in;
-      west facing: no sun in the morning, sun in the afternoon and   evening, lots of wind, particularly in the chilly and damp   autumn, lots of rain driving in.

In addition, possible shelter provided by existing vegetation or buildings can also be considered. It makes some difference if you live in the middle of a village or town or in the open countryside.

If you live in an exposed place, the north facing situation is the least suitable. The south has its advantages as you have the maximum profit from the sun. However, one disadvantage is that the temperature in the aviary can become very high.
Personally, an east facing situation suits me very well. The birds get the sun early, and although it disappears in the afternoon the warmth is held for quite some time. The prevailing west wind causes few problems, which is a great advantage particularly in autumn and winter. One disadvantage is the bitter east wind in winter. However, this does

not blow so very often, and if it does I shut the birds up in the shelter, so that they are not troubled by it.

For a west facing situation the same applies in the main as for east, but then the other way round. In this case a number of the disadvantages can be overcome by covering part of the flight.

Besides the climate there are a number of other aspects which have to be worked into the whole. For example a good view of the aviaries from the house has its positive side. Another point is the prevailing peace and quiet. At night it is to be recommended that the birds are not disturbed by noise, lights (for example from car headlights) and such like, although experience has taught us that birds are able to adjust fairly easily, especially if there is some regularity in the disturbance.

In the end every enthusiast must list all the possibilities and impossibilities for his own situation, and in doing so he must of course not forget that the finances can also play an important role.

Before you actually begin to build, gather information from as many other aviculturists as possible. See how they have built and ask anything which is not clear to you. And when doing so do not forget the most important question: what would you change if you had to build it again? Because although it is possible to learn from pleasant experiences, you can perhaps learn even more from unpleasant ones.

The general view that you will get from aviculturists is that there is one generally accepted standard construction: flights one meter wide, in rows next to each other, with or without separate passages through the shelters and/or flights. Vegetation is usually placed outside the aviary, mostly because many parakeets would destroy most of it. However, with the smaller species it is often not such a problem.

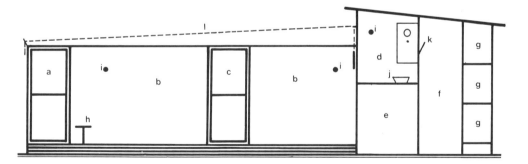

Possible construction for an aviary:

a. passage in front of the flights	g. cage
b. outside flight	h. water container
c. door from flight to flight	i. perch
d. shelter	j. feed container
e. storage space or room for small flight	k. inspection door in nest-box
f. passage in the shelter	l. nylon cord for closing shelter

Shelters

Before beginning to design the shelter you must consider which functions it must fulfil in your case. The following tips can be used.
The shelter can fulfil the following functions:
  - night accommodation
  - accommodation during cold winter days
  - breeding and rearing young
  - providing feed and such like.

It is advisable to let the birds always spend the night inside. Parakeets cannot see well in the dark and are easily frightened. So if they spend the night outside they can take fright for all sorts of reasons (for example cats, owls, headlights) and take to the air in panic. Then they fly into the wire mesh at a considerable speed and as a result can receive all sorts of injuries, up to and including a broken neck. Therefore it is important that the shelter is built in such a way that it can be closed, for there are always birds that, even after they have been chased inside, fly out again.
The closing can best be done from outside the aviary, for example by means of a length of nylon cord going over the aviary to the shelter, where it can be attached to a hatch which can drop down between two aluminium strips. Do not make this hatch too light, otherwise it will not fall sufficiently well, and do not make it from a material on which the birds like to chew.
Some aviculturists have such a cord running through the flight; this is not always such a good idea, as some birds will bite into it.
Birds like to sleep as high up as possible. Therefore if you build the shelter higher than the flight many of them will tend to go inside at night by nature. If that is not the case, they can be shut up completely for a period of one to three weeks and after that they are usually so used to it that they go in of their own accord.

The shelter provides against the effects of all types of bad weather, but also against strong sunlight. What is more, it offers the necessary peace and quiet.
By nature parakeets are most active in the morning and in the evening, because they have to fill their stomachs after and before the night. During the day therefore they are usually fairly inactive; this is particularly important in Australia as it can become very hot then and there is little point in wasting a lot of energy in the high temperatures. Therefore many parakeets here sit inside for a large part of the day. You must make sure that no draughts can get into the shelter, because parakeets are very sensitive to them.

During cold winter days it is sometimes advisable to shut the birds up. Although Australian parakeets are not among those most susceptible to frost, it is certainly no fun for them to have to brave the low temperatures which sometimes occur here. The closing of the shelter alone ensures that the temperature inside remains higher than outside, chiefly because the wind can no longer blow in.
Although for the other functions mentioned the size of the shelter does not need to be so great, this stay during the winter could be a reason to make it a little bigger so that the birds can fly round a bit. Exercise is after all a good way of keeping warm.
Another point which should be considered is the possible installation of heating. Most aviculturists do not consider it essential for parakeets but, even so, the birds will not enjoy temperatures of more than twenty degrees C below zero. Moreover, under these conditions

5. *Part of the author's aviary complex*

it is also no fun for the keeper to supply food and drink. A little heating also drives out the unhealthy chilly, damp air and prevents the drinking water from freezing.

This will not only make it more pleasant for the birds and their keeper, but also reduce the risk of sickness and death. Every aviculturist with any experience will agree that cases of sickness and death increase in cold and wet periods; from October to March the numbers are much higher than in the rest of the year.

It can therefore only be a good thing if the birds are protected against biting winds, fog, drizzle and driving rain.

If you do consider some form of heating, take into account the fact that paraffin and oil are the least healthy, that electricity is relatively expensive, and that gas offers the most advantages. Of course, best of all is to have it connected to the central heating.

If the aviary still has to be built, put down a number of pipes just in case; perhaps you will never use them but if you should change your mind later it will be fairly simple to connect them. Consider water (+ waste), electricity and heating.

If you can convince your birds to breed inside, that can only have advantages. It is much quieter than outside, night visitors can do little evil, the breeding process is easier to check, and the temperature is more even. If a nest-box hangs outside, rainwater can possibly run in and strong sunlight on it can raise the temperature inside much too high.

Finally, the feed containers are placed in the shelter. Not only are they unaffected by the weather there, but it is also handiest for you as keeper as you will usually store your feed there and you yourself will not be bothered by the weather.

It is also handy to lay on water. It will be an advantage when cleaning and possibly when providing drinking water. The latter can be particularly useful during periods of frost. If you otherwise provide water outside, it is easier to do it inside during these periods because then it will not freeze. Moreover, you will have to do this if you shut your birds up for a longer period.

An electricity supply will provide the lighting needed and if necessary a hospital cage can be connected.

Particulary with a large number of aviaries, a passage running behind the shelters is essential. This is very efficient and saves time when tending the birds. You might even consider making the birdroom so deep that you can have a passage in the middle, with on the one side the shelter and beyond the flights, and on the other side a space of 50 to 60cm for placing cages.

Do not make the doors from the passage to the shelters any bigger than is strictly necessary. If there is too much space at the side or top of an open door, there are quite a number of birds that could have the tendency to fly past you, especially if they cannot go outside. The solution is, therefore, not too big a door, or a small door for feeding and another bigger one for activities like cleaning, placing nest-boxes, catching birds and so on.

Personally I have the floor of the shelter at a height of about one meter. As the surface area is about one by one meter, it is not necessary to use the entire space between the ground and the ceiling. After all, the birds do not fly vertically, and they as good as never land on the floor of a shelter. The raising of the floor has at least two advantages: firstly the room is very easy to keep clean because everything can be done without bending down (however the surface area should not exceed one by one as otherwise you cannot reach everywhere); secondly the remaining space underneath can be put to all sorts of other uses, for example storing seed, nest-boxes and such like, or even for making flights for smaller birds.

The partitions that I have between the shelters and the passage are of wire mesh. Although the birds are therefore able to see each other, I do not have the impression that this causes problems; neighbouring pairs soon get used to each other. What is more, you can make sure that the most aggressive species are placed some distance apart. An advantage of this construction is that the birds can see you coming when you have to visit the birdrooms; in a closed space they hear something but do not know what it is, and this can make them a little restless. Furthermore it is an advantage by the installation of lighting and heating. One or two lamps in the passage can light everywhere; with closed shelters this is not possible. The same goes for the heating: if it is installed in the passage the warmth spreads throughout all the shelters. You do not even need to lay pipes or wires through the shelters. If they are there for some reason or other, make sure that the birds cannot get at them, for otherwise there are bound to be accidents.

If the heating is being used in winter, do not have it higher than a couple of degrees above zero; otherwise the difference with the temperature outside will become too great, which can cause the birds to go into moult.

Flight

The flight is attached to the shelter and constructed entirely of wire mesh. The width at that end is the same as the shelter. This is usually one meter, mainly because this is the standard width of wire mesh. If this size is taken into account during designing and building, it will save a lot of work regarding cutting and attaching. The wire most used in Holland has a mesh of 19 x 19mm and a thickness of 1,05mm. New mesh tends to glisten brightly, particularly when the sun shines on it. You can prevent this by going over it with creosote using a roller or brush; this shows the birds to their best advantage.

The frame of the flight is constructed from wood, the reasons being that it is cheapest and that the wire can easily be attached to it. A disadvantage is that some parakeets start chewing it. This can be prevented by attaching the mesh to both inside faces of the woodwork in one flight, and in the one next it to both outside faces; then next to that on the inside, and so on. The chewing birds are then placed in the flights where the mesh is on the inside. Double mesh is of course better still.

Another possibility is to use metal for the frame. This is much more expensive and the mesh is more difficult to attach, but it is long-lasting and it does not get chewed.

If you have a number of flights, there are various possibilities regarding accessibility. Firstly you can make a passage along the front of the flights; this means that you cannot reach the birds directly from outside because of the passage in between. A second possibility is to place doors in the partitions between the flights. This can be done at either end; however, this is not advisable because, if the door goes completely to the top, a perch cannot be placed there but will have to be moved further inside, which unnecessarily limits the amount of flying space for the inhabitants. If the door does not go to the top, a perch can be placed but then there will always be droppings in the place where you have to pass. Therefore it is best to place the doors in the middle of the flight. Make sure that the fastenings are sturdy, because parakeets are inquisitive by nature: it would not be the first time if they popped round to see the neighbours.

The water containers can be fixed to the front of the flights; if they are on the ground they get dirty much more quickly than when they are placed a little higher. In this position they can be easily filled with a watering can or a hosepipe. It is even worth considering making a flap in the mesh through which they can also be cleaned from outside. In any case, make sure that they are not placed under the perch as the birds will fill them with their droppings.

Some aviculturists cover their aviaries completely, some partly, and others not at all. The first mentioned have the advantage that the birds are not bothered by worms; moreover, it provides a certain amount of protection. A disadvantage is that a sort of greenhouse effect can develop in hot weather.

If only a section is covered, the birds can sit outside without being bothered by the less pleasant weather conditions like burning sun, heavy rain, and wind. They can then choose for themselves: in the open outside, under shelter outside, or inside. In this case it is often the section adjoining the shelter which is covered.

During construction the fact that roofing from corrugated plastic and glass filters out the ultraviolet rays from the sun should be taken into account, because this restricts the production of vitamin D.

With complete or partial covering it is less inadvisable to hang the nest-boxes outside.

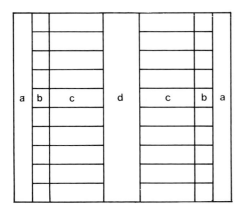 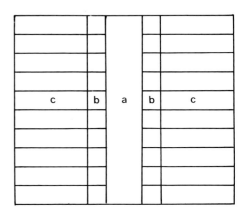

Two plans of larger aviary complexes:
a. passage in the shelter
b. shelter
c. outside flight
d. passage along the front of the flights

Other inhabitants

The aviary is intended for the housing of parakeets. However, you are always confronted with other unintended inhabitants and animals that have got it in for your birds. This applies mainly to mice and cats, and to a lesser degree animals such as moles, rats, weasels, owls and other birds of prey. There are also the less noticeable invaders such as bloodlice and other insects.

One of the worst plagues can be mice. They manage to get into nearly any aviary. If they are not too big they can get through the standard 19 x 19mm mesh, and the smallest of holes in the birdroom is often big enough. Therefore always build with mice at the back of your mind. Close everything off as well as possible and make sure there are no dark corners, because that is what they prefer. Keep everything inside open and light. If you are going to install insulation (for example in the roof), make sure that they can never get to it. Because once they do it is extremely difficult to get them out again, and they are capable of chewing the material into tiny pieces whereby its effect is completely lost. Particularly tempex is a hopeless material in this respect. There is a chance that you will find it strewn throughout the aviary. Then there is only one consolation: you are not the first to whom this has happened.

Box in which to lay mouse poison. They are attracted to this because it is dark

Mice can be exterminated with various traps and with poison.

If the same poison is constantly used, there is a chance that they will become immune to it. This means that a different sort must occasionally be used. This can be set down in open dishes out of the reach of the birds. For application in the shelter small boxes with a narrow opening can be used. If a brick is laid on top of it the birds will not be able to do anything with it. Be careful with this, however, for it appears that the mice sometimes carry the grains about. If you happen to discover that the mice always walk along the same route, for example along a wall, just place an old-fashioned mousetrap there; they often walk straight over it and bait is not even necessary.

Another possibility is to place almost completely closed boxes. If there are no other dark places, there is a good chance that they will sleep in them. Once they are inside it is easy to close the box, and the following step needs no explanation.

I will not have to tell you much about cats. The most effective method is to install an electric fence. There are installations on the market which have been specially developed for the aviculturist. The installations used in farming for cattle fencing is also suitable. These are sometimes available secondhand at reasonable prices.

Placing double mesh prevents cats from getting at the birds, but the effects of the fright remain.

After a time cats often come to realise that they cannot get at the birds; they then hardly even glance at them. This is also true for the birds: they often get to know the cats that are regularly in the neighbourhood. However, if a stranger comes along that acts a little differently, all hell breaks loose.

Moles, rats, weasels, and stoats can get into the aviary if the foundations are not deep enough, or the mesh of the wire is too big, or if the wire mesh does not fit closely. If you get weasels or stoats in this will inevitably cost you birds. So here also applies that prevention is better than cure. If anything does happen, it is often only due to your own carelessness.

Birds of prey can sit on top of the aviary or dive-bomb it. The greatest danger this can bring is fright, with all its attendant consequences.

It seems that owls can be frightened off at night by placing white glass balls on top of the aviary.

Bloodlice and other insects can be controlled by good hygiene and if necessary by insecticides. Creatures such as bloodlice are hardly ever noticed during quick inspections because they often spend their time in cracks and crannies. If you should notice them, take direct action.

IV. Purchasing

Which species

When deciding which species you are going to buy, of particular importance are: personal preference, experience, space, and finances.

Personal preference is extremely objective; one person is dead set on a Splendid, another on a King Parakeet. There is an extremely wide choice, as will become apparent later in Chapter IX, in which a complete overview is given of all the Australian parakeets which can be found in our aviaries. However, do not let yourself be tempted by a beautiful photo, but consider all the possibilities by visiting as many aviculturists as you can and studying the birds at your leisure. Ask as much as possible about their experiences with them, let it all sink slowly in and do not make any hasty decisions.

Not all species are equally easy to care for and breed. Therefore experience plays an important role. Use your common sense and do not begin straight away with the difficult (and therefore often the most expensive) species if you have not yet had any. Gain the necessary experience with birds which in general do not present any problems. The following lists of the (sub)species dealt with in this book might be of some help in this. The birds have been divided into four groups, of which A is the easiest and D the most difficult. You must see this as a general guide, because it is not possible to make sharp distinctions and the groups flow into each other.

Group A

Cockatiel
Eastern Rosella
Stanley Parakeet
Red-rumped Parakeet
Many-coloured Parakeet
Red-fronted Kakariki

Yellow-fronted Kakariki
Bourke's Parakeet
Blue-winged Grass Parakeet
Elegant Grass Parakeet
Turquoisine Grass Parakeet
Splendid Grass Parakeet

Group B

Barraband Parakeet
Rock Pebbler Parakeet
Princess of Wales Parakeet
Pennant's Parakeet

Yellow Rosella
Adelaide Rosella
Mealy Rosella

Group C

King Parakeet
Crimson-winged Parakeet
Red-capped Parrot
Barnard's Parakeet
Cloncurry Parakeet
Port Lincoln Parakeet

Twenty eight Parakeet
Yellow-bellied Rosella
Yellow-vented Blue-bonnet
Red-vented Blue-bonnet
Hooded Parakeet
Swift Parakeet

Group D

Green-winged King Parakeet
Amboina King Parakeet
Blue-cheeked Rosella
Brown's Parakeet

Naretha Blue-bonnet
Golden-shouldered Parakeet
Horned Parakeet

The next point is the available space. This determines to a certain extent which birds you can keep. Australian parakeets are active birds which like to fly. It is also good for their physical condition if they can get a lot of exercise. The general guide-line that the length of the aviary must increase with the length of the bird should be applied. A minimum length of two meters should be used for Neophemas and the like. For the larger species such as King and Crimson-winged Parakeets, five meters is the minimum. In older books and magazines it is stated that Kings must have a flight of at least eight meters long; although this is not strictly necessary, it must be said that this shows such birds to their best advantage. A large flying area lends the birds, and therefore also the hobby, extra beauty.

Nowadays the finances form much less of a limiting factor than they did a few years ago. The majority of the species described in this book are gradually becoming more than just a pipe dream or pie in the sky for many birdkeepers; most of them become obtainable sooner or later.

There are of course always exceptions such as the Horned Parakeet, the Naretha Blue-bonnet, the Golden-shouldered, and the Blue-cheeked Rosella, but when we consider what we have experienced with other species, the numbers of these will undoubtedly grow and this will cause the prices to drop.

When purchasing birds belonging to this group, you hardly need to take into account the noise that they make; it is not unpleasant and in some cases it is even melodious, the Red-rumped and the Pennant's for example. What is true is that the parakeets become active as soon as the sun comes up and also let themselves be heard. Not everybody will appreciate being woken up early in the morning by whistling parakeets. In emergencies this can be avoided by shutting them up in the evening and letting them out again in the morning at a 'respectable' time.

Which individuals

When you have decided which species you would like to have, the next question is which birds you should buy. The most important advice with regard to this is: buy preferably young birds. They will adjust themselves easiest to your aviary, feed, care and so on, and also to a new mate. Especially if you buy from reputable breeders you will get good birds which will give you years of enjoyment.

In many cases you will never know exactly where you are with older birds. They might be rejects, aggressive, egg-eaters, feather-pluckers, etc. That is of course not necessarily the case, but the reality is that the birds which for some reason or other do not appeal to their owners are the first to be got rid of. And the possible shortcomings are usually not visible on the outside. If you nevertheless do decide to buy older birds, do it from a reputable dealer.

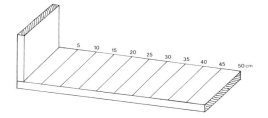

If you want to know if your birds are the correct length you can use this measuring board. Lay the bird with its head against the vertical piece and then you can read the length off at the tail

A disadvantage with young birds is that it is sometimes difficult to see the difference between the cock and the hen, and in some cases you will have to wait until they are two or more years old before they can start breeding. Bear in mind, however, that older birds need a settling-in period which can be just as long. And if that is the case, the advantage is lost. Moreover, you can be certain about the age of young birds and often not about older ones. A ring bearing a year is in this regard not always as reliable as it should be. Never buy birds which are related to each other, so never two birds out of the same nest, unless you can do the same somewhere else and form unrelated pairs by mixing them. Either buy two birds from one place and exchange one of them somewhere else, or only buy one bird from each place. Choose the biggest one with the best plumage. If there are a number of young from the same brood flying around, with some patience it is often possible to tell the cocks from the hens. In any case take your time for this.

When purchasing look out for clean and clear eyes; strong and healthy legs, toes, claws, and beak; power in the wings; clean nostrils; a good amount of flesh round the breastbone; and a fully-developed plumage. Do not worry if the feathers do not look too good; a shower of rain or the next moult will solve that problem. If, however, there is something missing in the plumage do not go ahead with the purchase. You never know if it will ever appear.

In addition to all this comes the best tool that an aviculturist can possess: the gift of being able to see if a bird is in top condition, ill, or healthy. This is above all a question of experience, and it can be expensive to gain that experience in our hobby.

If you wish to purchase mutations, take the above mentioned points likewise into account, but also make sure that you know beforehand which genetic rules apply. Think before buying a single mutation or split bird; first try to find out what sort of mate would be most suitable, whether you can get one easily and at a reasonable price, and what the result is likely to be.

How many

Most aviculturists tend to purchase as many species as possible. This is very understandable and it does not raise any problems, particularly with the commoner species.
Nevertheless, it is better to have at least two pairs of each species. For then there are always two unrelated birds available for selling if both pairs have chicks, there is more chance of getting chicks with two pairs, and if one bird dies, it can always be replaced by a chick from the remaining pair.

If you buy young birds, it is best to choose two cocks and two hens which are not related to each other. The four of them can then be placed in one aviary. If you have difficulty telling them apart, this can be solved by marking them with a felt-tip or cutting a bit off the tail feathers. However, it is often possible to discover some slight difference; usually no two birds are exactly the same: the sizes vary, the heads are different, one has a claw missing, another has a crooked claw, there is a feather out of place, or whatever.
As soon as you notice that two birds are becoming interested in each other, remove the other two.
The more young birds that are bought and placed together, the more chance of good breeding pairs. Make sure that there are not more than two birds in one aviary for longer than is strictly necessary, particularly with the more aggressive species.
If you want to build up a good breeding stock, you should follow the example of the keepers of Budgerigars and Canaries, who breed various pairs and always keep the best chicks for further breeding.

Where

There are a number of possibilities for the purchasing of birds: at a bird sale, through an advertisement in a paper or bird magazine, from a dealer or a well-known aviculturist; you can even have someone else buy the birds for you.

A bird sale is not the most suitable occasion. The inferior birds that are around - and always will be - are found here more than anywhere. Possible defects are also often less noticeable, and the impression you get of the size of a bird in a cage or box is very different than in an aviary. There is nothing to beat purchasing a young bird which is still flying round with its parents in the breeder's aviary. This could be at a breeder known to you, but it is also possible to find such birds through advertisements. When buying from a dealer, first ask experienced aviculturists if this is advisable.
Only have someone else buy a bird for you if you are sure that he has the necessary experience and is acting in good faith. If you are still inexperienced and are going to purchase a bird, take an experienced aviculturist with you. First try to make the choice

yourself and have him confirm it. That way you can see for yourself whether you are beginning to get an eye for it.

And remember that the most important thing is not to make any hasty decisions. If you are not sure whether to buy a bird or not, do not do it!! For then there is apparently something which you do not quite like about it; prevent coming to regret it later. Only the best birds are good enough.

Particularly in the beginning many people find it quite difficult to back out of the sale in such a case, but the more experienced you become the easier it gets to make such decisions.

When

The best time to purchase birds is shortly after the end of the breeding season, when the birds are independent. You can choose the best looking young birds then, and they will have ample opportunity to adjust before the start of the new breeding season. This is of special importance if they are sexually mature after only one year.

An added advantage is that the birds are then at their cheapest. Experience has shown that the prices rise as the new breeding season approaches. The supply is smaller and the risky winter period is over then.

Separate bought birds as much as possible during transport, as this gives the least chance of accidents and injuries. Put them in their new aviary preferably in the morning, so that they have as much daylight as possible available in which to orientate themselves and to discover where the perches, feed and drink containers are. Shut them up in the shelter for the first couple of days so that they become familiar with it, and have to spend the night there. After that the entrance to the flight can be opened.

Naturally, birds can be bought at any time of the year. However, instant breeding success should not be expected then in all cases; this depends to some extent on the time of purchase and the age of the birds. The closer to the beginning of the breeding season, the less chance of immediate results. Of course results are never completely ruled out; after all, most Australian parakeets have by now adjusted to life in captivity and to our climate.

Newly obtained birds can be released together into their new home without much risk. If, however, a bird has been bought that has to be put in with another one already present, be careful when it concerns, particularly older, birds which might be aggressive. Do not put a hen straight in with an aggressive cock; he could pursue and (mortally) injure her. First put them next to each other for a time so that they can get acquainted, or try to arrange that the hen can adjust to the aviary first and the cock be released some time later.

Bear in mind that aggression is in fact part of an instinctive behaviour pattern that has developed in the wild as a result of the competition for limited resources such as food, suitable mates, nest-sites, and territories; these are all preconditions for the survival of the species. Therefore, take this into account when building up your collection, and note well that the competition for hens is the greatest source of aggression.

V. Care and management

One of the most important aspects of keeping and breeding birds is a good diet. When you begin you should realise that you have the responsibility to create conditions which approach as near as possible those in the wild. It stands to reason that it is not possible to supply exactly the same food. Therefore, substitutes have to be sought, the quality of which should be high and of mixed variety.

As a result of the enormous boom in bird-keeping it has become an interesting market for the animal feed industry. All kinds of prepared feed are on the market, which makes it fairly easy for you. Through these developments it has also become possible to carry out scientific research into the needs of the various species of birds; although it is probably true that these will never be known. The experiences of various aviculturists have also become an integral part of this research. If in the old days it was sometimes a little amateurish, nowadays there are many who delve deeply into the background of bird-keeping and make contributions which can be of benefit to others.

It is not my intention to tell extensively about theories on diet here. Experience has shown that the average enthusiast is helped more by as practical an approach as possible, in which the why? is often considered less important than the what? People who are interested in the background will be able to find sufficient literature available to them.

Nutrients

The nutrients that your parakeets need in their diet are proteins, carbohydrates, fats, vitamins, minerals, and water.

Proteins make up about half of the dry weight in the bodies of humans and animals; in plants it is often much less. Proteins are involved in all the important processes in the living world. The birds need them in order to grow and to develop their plumage; in older birds they are used for the renewal of cells.

During their rearing there is a greater need for proteins than in winter, when they have a rest period. So before they start developing a new plumage for winter, the extra proteins are required because the plumage is built up from them.

Proteins are made up of a great number of small building blocks called amino acids. The bird can produce some of these itself, others have to be present in the diet. The nutritional value of protein is dependent on the content of the essential amino acids, these are the ones which the parakeet is not able to produce itself. Many vegetable proteins are low on these. A source of animal proteins must therefore be provided.

Carbohydrates supply the energy necessary for living and consequently they are one of the most important elements in the diet of humans and animals. They come mainly from vegetable sources. Carbohydrates do not play any part in the renewal of cells, but in movement and body temperature. Cereals and seeds contain many carbohydrates, in the form of starch; sugars also belong to this group.

Fats (and oils) also supply energy, give protection, and can also be stored as a reserve. Particularly as winter approaches it can be a good thing for your birds to have a little extra fat in their bodies. Not only is this good insulation but the birds can also use it in times of need.

Vitamins are necessary in small quantities to sustain the bird's body and keep it functioning normally. They do not supply any energy but they are essential to life. Parakeets must receive them in order to make breeding and growth possible, and to remain healthy. They must be taken in with the food, and are used in the production and breaking up of proteins, carbohydrates, and fats. Vitamins occur in nature in various forms; nowadays, however, they are manufactured artificially in great quantities. The nutritional value of these is the same.

Minerals are inorganic or non-living materials which the birds use for growth and replacement. Of particular importance are calcium, phosphoros, sodium, manganese, copper, potassium, iron, and iodine. These all have their own function.
The term spore element is used for minerals of which the birds need very little.

Little needs to be said about the importance of water. It accounts for more than half of the bird's bodyweight. You might notice that not all parakeets drink the same amount. A reason for this could be that the birds from dry areas are more able to make use of the liquid in the food they eat.

Besides the above mentioned nutritional elements, grit and gravel are also essential. Grit, and cuttlefish, can supply the birds with the calcium they need for the production of eggshells and bones. Therefore, attention must be paid to this especially during the breeding season and the moult.
The gravel's function is to grind the food in the stomach. Therefore, it is not digested in the body, but when the sharp edges have been rounded off, the remains are deposited in the droppings.

Standard diet

Now that an outline has been given of what your parrotlikes will need in order to lead a healthy life, it is time to consider how this can be related to the birds' diet.
It is not feasible for the individual aviculturist to compose a diet of percentages and ratios, which exactly meets the needs of the birds. You are reliant on what the market has to offer and what you can get out of the wild or the vegetable garden. Because of the boom in the keeping of parakeets as a hobby, it has become lucrative for the trade to get into this market, and, as a result, numerous products have appeared during the last few years.

You can ensure that there are no deficiencies in your parakeets' diet if you stick to the following menu:
a.   a seed mix. There is a variety of seed mixes available which form the basic ingredients;
b.   a soft food. It is not necessary to make this yourself. The quality of the available ready-mixed products is generally good. It is important that this is the part of the diet in which your birds get animal protein; they cannot do without it;

c. fruit and greens. These provide many vitamins and minerals. This includes all sorts of vegetables, but also weeds and wild berries;
d. fresh branches. These are not only of good nutritional value but also supply a diversion for the birds. They are particularly keen on willow branches;
e. gravel for grinding food in the stomach;
f. grit, mainly for the calcium requirement;
g. bathing and drinking water.

With regard to the supplementary feed you can use your imagination; various food sources from the wild, the vegetable garden, and fruit trees are admirably suitable. Make sure that you do not take too much from road verges, as the exhaust fumes settle on what is growing there and this can lead to symptoms of poisoning. It goes without saying that this also applies to sprayed foodstuffs.
The more variety in your birds' diet the better. If you pay enough attention to this, it is not necessary to resort to all sorts of vitamin preparations, and other mixtures and substances. Your birds can extract these from the food that you supply them with. Remember that an overdose is also damaging.

The importance of the variation mentioned was shown in a year-long study into the feeding habits of the Eastern Rosella made in the wild in Australia. It appeared that they made use of grasses, herbs, bushes and trees. They ate from no less than 82 different species!
This also highlights the fact that the Australian parakeets are for the most part vegetarians; they are chiefly dependent on vegetable foods. They do, however, need some animal foodstuffs, among other things, protein; this they get chiefly in the form of insects, many of which are found in the berries and other fruits which they eat.

Besides the normal seed the birds can also be supplied with germinated seeds. To do this a quantity of seed is put in water for 24 hours. Then it is rinsed and placed in a warm position in a virtually closed container. Depending on the temperature it will start germinating after one or two days. It is a good idea to rinse the seeds clean occasionally to prevent the growth of mould. The nutritional value is at its highest when the shoots are between one and two millimetres long.

In winter the parakeets can certainly do with some extra oily seeds (for example sunflower seeds); it gives a bit more protection against the low temperatures.
If it freezes, the drinking water will as often as not turn into ice. The first thing is then to supply fresh water as regularly as possible. If it has snowed, many birds will soon discover that it is edible and also quenches their thirst.
If there is no snow you can break up the ice in the drink containers or scrape a layer off. There is a fair chance that your parakeets will pick some up. They generally like to chew on a chunk of ice. I regularly see them in my aviaries with pieces in their claws.
Sometimes a bird will start playing with its drink container. This can be avoided by putting a stone in it or by jamming it in somewhere.

If they will not eat grit out of a container, you can scatter it over the floor: this often solves the problem.
There is little point in giving charcoal in cases of (for example) watery droppings. The charcoal is not digested. As it is fairly porous it absorbs various substances which are important to the bird, and as the charcoal leaves the body again in the droppings every-

thing that has been taken up in it is no longer of any value. Because it also absorbs liquid the droppings may well look better, but of course this does not cure the actual cause of the problem.

Then finally a word about the parakeets' use of their feet. You will undoubtedly have noticed that some birds hold food in their feet and some do not, and that some scratch their heads directly and others do it round the back of a wing. In general it is true that the species which look for the majority of their food on the ground seldom hold it in their feet; birds which live more in the trees do. Furthermore, most 'tree-birds' scratch their heads directly, whereas 'ground-birds' do this round the back of a wing.

A separate aspect concerns the age which your birds can reach if well cared for. Unfortunately relatively little is known about this. Below I list a number of figures which I came across during the preparation for this book. You should not take it for granted that these are average ages; certainly not all birds will reach them.

Cockatiel	28 years old
Crimson-winged Parakeet	30 years old
Rock Pebbler Parakeet	17 years old
Princess of Wales Parakeet	35 years old
Pennant's Parakeet	19 years old
Eastern Rosella	28 years old
Bourke's Grass Parakeet	18 years old
Swift Parakeet	15 years old (caught in the wild and therefore older)

Management

We have to be fully aware that, as their keepers, the birds are entirely dependent upon us for their welfare. By keeping them in an aviary we take the duty upon us to guarantee them a good life. Every bird is an individual and as such deserves the necessary attention. The keeper must therefore take the time to get to know each bird separately.
For example, on purchasing one parakeet is wilder than another. This is partly dependent on its character, but also to a certain extent on the influence of the surroundings. A bird which is housed in a very quiet place and which sees few people will be much shyer than one which constantly sees people walking past its aviary. The clearest examples of this are zoos and bird parks, in which there is often no question of any shyness, not even of the imported birds. In such a situation they completely lose their fear. This also has consequences for breeding: tame parakeets will breed and rear their young more easily and peacefully than shy ones.

This is why it can do no harm to allow a lot of people to walk past your birds, particularly out of the breeding season. From my own experience I can even go so far as to say that after some time playing children hardly have any effect on their behaviour; of course they must not get too close to the aviaries. The main advantage is that your birds will be more steady and less likely to fly into the birdroom in these situations, so that you can enjoy them in the open air more frequently.

Set out with the idea of developing regular habits; this gives your birds a certain sense of familiarity and recognition. Feed at fixed times; they will get used to it and after a while they will be, as it were, ready to welcome you at all times. Always let them hear you are coming. This is of particular importance in the birdroom, as they will not always be able to see you. If you talk or whistle to them they will know that you are around; that is better than hearing a vague shuffling of feed containers or unknown footsteps.

Parakeets are not only able to recognize their keeper by hearing, but also by sight. My wife is sometimes able to tell that I have come home by the sound of the birds. Furthermore, do everything as quietly as possible and do not make any unexpected movements.

No aviculturist will be able to avoid having to catch a parakeet now and then. For your relationship with the birds it is of course a good thing to limit this as much as possible. But in cases of sickness, worming, moving, or selling you will nevertheless have to face it. Keep the catching time as short as possible. Be sure of yourself and do not become uncertain, because then it can take a long time and both the bird and the keeper will get agitated. Keep the catching net hidden for as long as possible, for the parakeets get to recognise this and feel that something is going to happen as soon as they see it.

If you grasp the bird firmly immediately it is in the net there will be no problems. If you get bitten it will usually be your own fault, because you have been too anxious and cautious. I am not in favour of using gloves, because then the direct contact with the bird's body is lacking and you cannot feel exactly whether you have got hold of it properly.

The inhabitants of our aviaries enjoy at least twelve hours daylight in their natural surroundings. This is different in our part of the world. In the winter here it can be that they sit in the dark from four in the afternoon till eight in the morning; so for sixteen hours. Therefore, they have to build up their reserves for those sixteen hours during daylight. And this is asking a lot, especially as they have a hard time of it any way due to the climate and temperature. During this period, therefore, food is all the more necessary, as it provides energy and body heat. It is therefore advisable to increase the number of hours of light artificially; the easiest way to do this is with the help of a time switch.

VI. Breeding

With the onset of the breeding season begins the most exciting period for the parakeet breeder. There is much to see and do; the birds awake as it were from their hibernation and develop all sorts of activities. The aviculturist must react to this by beginning in good time with the supply of more protein-rich food than in the winter rest period, making nest-boxes available, and to ensure the necessary quiet.

Especially light and to a lesser extent temperature influence the reproductive cycle. In the wild an important stimulus for the awakening of the breeding instinct is formed by a combination of an abundance of food and favourable weather conditions. In Australia, therefore, the start of the breeding period is heavily dependent on the rain seasons. The eggs are often layed one or two weeks after the first rainfall. The closer the birds live to the equator in the wild the less they react to the changes in the length of the days. This can be explained by the fact that in the tropics there is little difference between the number of hours of darkness and daylight throughout the year. The availability of food is therefore the most important factor there.

Seen in this light it is no coincidence that some of the most successful aviary birds (Budgerigar, Cockatiel, Zebra Finch) come from the same area: they feed mainly on grass seeds and breed after the rain season when there is an abundance of seeds. In that respect they could actually have eggs at any time of the year here.

We find an insensitivity for the number of hours of daylight in, for example, the Hooded Parakeet and the Brown's Parakeet, birds which come from the extreme (tropical) north of Australia. They breed there in a fairly wet period and also stick to that here, which means that they only become active from September onwards. Only recently have there ocassionally been pairs which have bred in our spring.

Generally speaking Australian parakeets dislike touching each other. You therefore hardly ever see them sitting close to each other on the perch; they always keep some distance. This aloofness must be overcome as the breeding season begins. The cock then has to try to approach the hen more closely. In this group of parakeets the problem is solved by the development of a courtship ceremony, which gradually allows him to cautiously come nearer to her. He stimulates her breeding instinct with his courtship behaviour and, what is more, he gets so carried away with his own performance that he forgets himself and as a result slowly overcomes his timidity.

His repertoire of movements is fairly limited. He can jump up and down, bend or stretch himself, sway his head from side to side, beat his wings, let his wings hang or hold them up, twist his body, widen his eyes, or dilate his pupils. Not all his movements are calming for the hen; some are downright aggressive, for example 'the jump in the air'. Although this might gain the hen's attention it also seems to be a warning to other cocks that the hen to which this behaviour is directed is no longer available.

Each species has developed its own display which is for the most part unique. Natural selection increases the effectiveness of this by seeing to it that the parts of the body displayed have become more colourful. A bright colour pattern in a particular place, therefore, gives us a clue regarding the courtship behaviour of each species; a good example of this is the Crimson-winged Parakeet.

The cocks that turn or bob their heads often have bright colours there; those that let their wings hang will often have brightly coloured coverts, and birds that hold their wings up display colours on their underside.

When in this manner the distance between the birds has been overcome mating will take place, after which the next steps in the reproduction cycle will follow.

Nest-boxes

All Australian parakeets found in our aviaries are hole-nesters. Most look for a hollow branch or trunk, often in a eucalyptus or gum-tree. This preference is due to the fact that these trees are hard on the outside but soft inside. If a branch breaks off the inside of the trunk rots away fairly quickly at that spot; the parakeet can also speed up this process by chewing.

A few (sub)species do breed in holes but hardly ever in trees: the Hooded and the Golden-shouldered Parakeet have a preference for termite hills, in which they themselves make tunnels with a nest-cavity at the end, during the rain season when the hills have become soft. However, in an aviary these (sub)species settle for nest-boxes.

The natural nest-site is therefore relatively easy to imitate. To begin with there are two possibilities: a natural log (a hollowed-out trunk), or a home-made nest-box of wood or (multiplex) sheets. A home-made box has various advantages:
-   as Australian parakeets have been bred here for centuries, they take to these fairly readily;
-   they are much lighter in weight;
-   if necessary you can adjust their shape to suit your aviary;
-   you can make them just how you want; for example you can even dictate the position of the entrance hole and the inspection flap.

Now, how big should a nest-box be? This is indicated separately in Chapter IX during the descriptions of each species. However, there is a general rule of thumb which can be applied. Assuming the bottom of the box is square, the sides of this should be the same length as the distance from the beak to the rectum of the bird to breed in it. This boils down to the length of the bird excluding the tail. The height of the box should then be three times this length. However, as this does not apply to all parakeets, for example not for the King Parakeets, it is better to rely on the sizes stated for each species.

Nest-boxes are often made too big. The smaller they are the more warmth they retain. In the wild the birds sometimes nest in the most impossibly small holes, in which the chicks are sometimes not even able to sit next to each other on the bottom, but hang halfway up the sides. That is not such a problem as these sides are always uneven and so contain enough footholds. In smaller nest-boxes the young are forced to sit against each other so that they keep each other warm.

Another disadvantage of too big a nest-box is that they let in too much light, which can prevent the birds from starting to breed. Many parakeets like to sit in the dark.

It is the generally accepted rule that the entrance hole should be just big enough for the bird to get through. Firstly this gives a feeling of security, and secondly no more light shines in than is strictly necessary. This is, however, not a hard and fast rule: in Australia parakeets do use considerably bigger holes in order to enter the nest cavity.

The holes in home-made boxes can be in the middle or to one side. An off-centre hole has the advantage that the light inside is unevenly distributed, which means that the hen can search out the darkest corner. The hole does not necessarily have to be round; there is no objection to a different shape.

As the sides of the box are often fairly smooth, it is a good idea to attach something to act like a ladder to the inside. This can be in the form of a piece of mesh, although with this it is not unheard of for the birds to get their claws or rings caught behind it. It is therefore better to hammer a couple of large staples into a side. You could also attach a couple of pieces of wood, but these can easily be chewed up.

Make sure that your parakeets can get into the nest-box without too much difficulty; place a perch under or near the entrance hole.

Various sizes of multiplex nest-boxes. Notice the mesh under the entrance hole and the inspection flap

You can hang up the nest-box in a variety of places, inside as well as outside. I prefer inside as this has a number of advantages:
- it is the quietest place. The chance of disturbance is smallest;
- no unpleasant things can occur at night which cause the bird to panic and leave the nest-box, with all the attendant consequences;
- the nest-box is little affected by weather conditions like late night-frosts, strong sunlight, or driving rain;
- inspection is much easier.

If you have a row of shelters with a passage running behind them, it is best to hang the box in the shelter on the wall between the shelter and the passage. If you then make a hole in the wall and place the inspection flap in the box, you can carry out inspections very easily and without entering the shelter; when doing this you must make sure that the hen is not sitting on the nest.

Should you nevertheless decide to hang the nest-box outside, ensure that it is in any case protected against strong sunlight and driving rain; if you have covered part of the flight, a position in this section is the most suitable.

If you buy new birds which still have to choose a nest-box, it is a good idea to hang up a couple of boxes so that they can make a selection.
However, in general Australian parakeets are not too choosy, mainly because they have been bred here for generations already. Therefore with the less difficult species you can take the chance of hanging only one box in the place that suits you best. Keep a good eye on it however; if at the beginning of the breeding period they do not pay any attention to it, hang up another one in a different place and possibly of a different shape. When buying young birds it is also a good idea to see in what kind of box they were reared; look particularly at the box out of which the hen has come and copy that.

Now a few words about the best time to hang up the box. There are two possibilities: either let it hang the whole year round, or only supply it at the approach of the breeding season. Both have their advantages and disadvantages.
If the boxes remain hanging the whole year (in which case they must of course be cleaned out after the breeding season), the birds can decide when they want to start nesting themselves, which is what they also do in the wild. A disadvantage to this is the risk of low temperatures and the possible return of night-frosts. This can result in egg-binding, or temporary or permanent loss of the urge to breed. Something which you must also watch out for is that certain species have become so domesticated by continuous breeding that they no longer stick to the seasons and in mild winters can start breeding. Examples of these are the Kakariki, the Cockatiel, and some Neophemas.
With these birds it is therefore a good idea to remove the boxes or to cover the entrance hole. If the birds get into the nest-box and you discover that there are eggs at a time that does not suit you, wait until the clutch is complete and then remove them. Then you can remove or close up the box.
Bird-keepers that hang the nest-boxes up just before the breeding season begins often choose the month of March. Some have a set date, but this can have its drawbacks. The date should partly depend on the weather and the way in which the birds react to it. For some birds March is already a bit on the late side: there are Blue-bonnets that already start breeding activities at the end of February. In such a case nest-boxes which are hung too

late can result in the breeding season having to be considered a failure.

An advantage can be that the birds cannot begin too early, thus ensuring that the risk of egg-binding, cold weather and suchlike is much smaller.

Regarding nesting material that can be used there are several possibilities: light soil mixed with rotting leaves or pine- needles, an upturned turf into which some sawdust has been beaten with the fist, rotten wood which the birds themselves can chew fine, coarse sawdust, etc. Do not use peat, fine sawdust, or any other fine material: this may cause dust which the chicks breathe in and with it mould spores which can lead to fungal infections. The nostrils can also become easily blocked.

When the nesting material is put into the box it should be slightly damp; this helps the development and hatching of the eggs.

Eggs

If all goes well, the birds accept the nest-box offered, courtship and pairing take place, and shortly afterwards the eggs are layed. The number varies with each species. The eggs are coloured white; they do not need to be camouflaged because they are layed in dark holes. Laying usually takes place in the late afternoon or early evening at intervals of forty-eight hours, i.e. every two days. As the hen starts brooding after the second or third egg, the first chicks hatch at about the same time and the rest of the clutch follows every 48 hours. Some breeders remove the first eggs to ensure that all the chicks hatch at about the same time. However, this is not necessary; after all, in the wild there is a difference in size, but there is sufficient food available to give all the young enough. In large clutches, however, the difference between the oldest and the youngest can sometimes be too big; which can prevent the progress of the youngest.

If the eggs are temporarily removed they must be turned several times a day. Research has shown that the hen does this about every half hour during the day and about every two or three hours at night: on average about twenty-four times a day. This prevents the embryo sticking to the shell membrane, which leads to death. Eggs must not be kept at too high a temperature, otherwise the embryo begins to develop.

If necessary the eggs can be marked by putting on a symbol or the date of laying in pencil. Ink and felt-tips can be damaging.

With all Australian parakeets only the hen broods, with the exception of the Cockatiel; they take turns. This is an indication that this bird is related to the cockatoos, because they do it as well.

It happens occasionally that the hen cannot release her egg. She will then sit hunched on the perch with a rounded rump. In many cases this can be cured by putting her into a warm place or by treating the cloaca with oil using a brush.

In eggs that have been brooded for at least five days you can see whether they are fertile by shining the light of, for example, a torch through them. A fertile egg shows red veins fanning out from the embryo to the wall of the yolk. Infertile eggs are translucent. Never throw away eggs that seem to be infertile. Maybe the hen has not been brooding for as long as you think. And besides, they might be of some use to the newly-hatched chicks: they retain warmth and offer some support.

Infertile eggs can be caused by a variety of reasons: birds which have a poor diet, are infertile, too young, either not simultaneouly sexually mature or in the mood to breed, not suitable for each other, or the cock is too aggressive.

If an egg shows signs of cracking it will dry out, which will lead to failure. This can be treated by brushing on a little (colourless) nail polish; no more than is strictly necessary. This seals the crack and prevents the egg drying out, if it has not been lying for too long. Generally there is not much point in opening eggs that have not hatched. Even assuming that the chick is still living at the time, in most cases they do not survive the operation. However, they are often dead already.

Some birds are egg eaters. There is not much to be done about this. If this is the case remove each egg as soon as possible after it has been laid and replace it with an artificial egg. Or give a bad egg or one filled with plaster in which you have mixed all sorts of hot substances such us mustard and pepper. The nasty taste may cure the bird of this irritating habit.
Sometimes it stops by itself once the hen starts to brood. Then you have to choose a suitable moment in which to put the original eggs back again.
Eggs which for one reason or the other cannot be left under the hen can first be kept for a number of days. However, tests with Cockatiels in America have shown that the germinative power begins to decrease after only three days and becomes doubtful after six. Therefore, it is better to place the eggs in an incubator after a couple of days. What happens then depends on a number of different factors.
It is best to place the eggs under the original hen again as soon as possible. If this is not possible you can see if there are any suitable foster parents. These have to be breeding at about the same time. The closer the species is related the better. And the difference in size must not be too great. Certain birds are extremely suitable as foster parents, for example Kakarikis and Red-rumped Parakeets. If this fails, perhaps there are bird-keeping friends to whom you can take your eggs.
The last possibility is to let the eggs hatch in the incubator and to hand-rear the chicks yourself. However, you have to realise what you are letting yourself in for. In the beginning the chicks have to be fed every couple of hours, also at night. For a number of weeks, therefore, you are hard at it the whole day and in this period you have to devote your entire time to the young parakeets.
The food is no longer the greatest problem in this period; there are now ready-made mixtures on the market. Make sure that the young get sufficient of everything, and particularly bear in mind the addition of grit.
The bird's stomach must learn how to deal with soft foods, otherwise things could go amiss when the bird has to fend for itself.
Everything considered there is nothing to beat young reared by their own parents. The parents can import something to them in feeding and behaviour that we as keepers are not able to. And it is not without reason that some chickens and quails as good as refuse to brood.

Now a word about the vitality of male sperm. It is not so that each egg has to be separately fertilised. Birds mate many times in order to increase the chance of fertile eggs as much as possible. The sperm from the male remains effective in the hen for several days and sometimes even for several weeks. Even if the cock is no longer in the company of the hen the clutch may nevertheless be fertilised. An illustration of this is the case of a pair of

Kings where the cock became so aggressive after the first egg had been laid that the owner had to separate them. The hen laid four eggs after this. Later it transpired that these last four of the clutch of five were all fertile.

The incubation periods for each species are given later in this book. There are no great differences between them. The climate can have a slight effect: this can mean that the eggs hatch a day late or a day early. Parrot-likes from dry areas often have a relatively short incubation period.

Chicks

As most species start breeding in March or April most young fly out during the period of May to July. On average the time between the first egg and leaving the nest is about two months. The hen does not sit for the first few days, then follows an incubation period of almost three weeks, and then the hatched young stay in the box for about another five weeks.

Parakeets are altricial birds, which means that the young birds have to be fed by the parents for some time before they can fend for themselves. For a few days after the chicks have hatched the hen hardly leaves the nest box, because the chicks cannot keep themselves warm.

The weight of a newly-hatched bird is about two-thirds of that of the egg; the chick therefore has a certain amount of food available to it so that it does not immediately have to be fed. If you are breeding inside with artificial lighting you must make sure that it is light for long enough. There must be plenty of time in which to feed the young. There is no point, however, in leaving the lights on for more than fourteen hours a day. Bear in mind that it must not become instantly dark. If a sitting hen or a hen with newly-hatched chicks happens to be off the nest for a while when the lights go out, she will not be able to find her way back, and then you can forget the clutch. Therefore always use dimmers and leave a five watt lamp on continuously in the birdroom.

After a week or ten days it is time to ring the young. This can be done in two ways: the first is to put the two most forward-facing toes through the ring first, the second is to include the longest backward-facing toe as well, so three forward and the shortest backward. Although, by the second method the joint is a bit bigger, this is still the easiest. The big advantage is that the ring only has to go a little way past this joint; if, by the first method, it has to go over the longest back toe difficulties can arise, particularly if you are a bit late.

Once the ring is on the leg, check to see if it will slide off again; if that is the case, wait a few days before trying it again.

One advantage of ringing your birds is that you can use them for identification purposes at a distance, thereby not having to catch the bird. And if you have two pairs of the same species, ring the young of one pair on the right leg and those of the other on the left. Then if it is necessary you can immediately take out an unrelated pair.

Normally speaking the parents see to it that the young birds reach the perch fit and healthy, if you supply a sufficient quantity of food. When the young birds leave the box for the first time they are extremely nervous and uncertain. And of course that is no

wonder in such a situation, for everything is new and unknown. When they enter the outside flight they could fly into the mesh at speed, because they do not know what it is and are unable to see it properly. It is wise to hang some branches or sacks against the mesh before they fly out to prevent this collision.

Furthermore, make sure that the young birds spend the night in the shelter. Making the acquaintance of a cat or bird of prey at night can have disastrous results.

After leaving the nest the young are fed by the parents for an even longer period. They have to learn to feed themselves gradually and must therefore remain with their parents for at least three weeks. And a little longer will do no harm. You should separate them if the parents start chasing the young birds or if a second clutch follows.

Many young birds have still got their immature plumage when they fly out. They normally moult in the first autumn, after which some species already get their adult plumage. Whether this is the case or not is related to sexual maturity. The later a species becomes sexually mature, the longer it takes before it takes on its adult plumage. A good moult is very important because then the young birds are well prepared for entering the difficult autumn and winterperiod.

Of course not all breeding periods go off perfectly. But do not instantly blame the birds if something goes wrong. First work out what exactly has gone wrong and what the reason could have been:
-    did you buy good quality birds;
-    are the birds sexually mature;
-    have the birds had time to get used to each other and their surroundings, and are they suited to each other;
-    have you really got a cock and a hen;
-    are the nesting conditions suitable;
-    have the birds been disturbed too much;
-    have the birds got any aggressive (related) neighbours which distracted them;
-    etc, etc.

45

Should you not find any clues in the answers to such questions, then have patience, and allow your birds the chance of another breeding season. Do not over hastily sell your parakeets and start forming new pairs. Not every pair reproduces on command and that's a good thing, because otherwise aviculture would lose some of its appeal.

You are only a true aviculturist when, despite the setbacks you may have had, you can laugh happily and keep going after each breeding season and winter!

VII. Mutations and genetics

During the last few years mutations have gradually become part and parcel of keeping Australian parakeets. Not so very long ago these were chiefly familiar in connection with the Cockatiel and the Red-rumped, and the few others were for the main part the preserve of a very small group of enthusiasts. The developments are going faster and faster and new mutations appear regularly. The consequences to aviculture of all this activity are not foreseeable; what is certain is that a whole new world is being opened.

Not everyone is equally enchanted with these mutations and many prefer to stick to the original normal-coloured birds. However, it would be a shortcoming in a book about Australian parakeets that did not deal with this subject, if only because the interest for it will undoubtably increase.

It is not my intention to do this in a complex and exhaustive manner. I have attempted to explain the most important principles as simply and practically as possible. This culminates at the end of the chapter in easy-reference summaries of a number of genetic rules which anybody should be able to apply after studying them for a while. Anybody who is not familiar with this subject should bear in mind that they will have to devote some time and attention to it in order to get the hang of it.

Colours

First of all we are going to look at the various colours that the feathers might have. This is fairly simple as we encounter only three forms, namely those with the pigments melanin and carotenoid, and those with the structural colour blue:

1. melanin: the dark pigments of feathers, beak, legs and claws, in other words the colours black, grey, and brown;
2. carotenoid: the colours yellow, orange, and red, which can be present in the feathers or the beak;
3. structural colour: blue (and violet). As the word structural suggests, the colour produced is related to the structure of the feather; the way in which the feather is built up.

You might have noticed that the colour green is not mentioned here. This is because green is not a primary colour but is produced by a combination of the pigment colour yellow and the structural colour blue. Therefore, if yellow disappears from a green bird then blue remains, and if blue is lost we get a yellow bird.

Mutations

In a simple approach the mutations can be traced back to changes in the melanin and carotenoid. Suchlike changes also occur in the structural colours, but so far this has hardly

47

ever been encountered in Australian parakeets. One example of this can be seen in the various dark forms and dark factors of the colour found in the *Agapornis roseicollis*: light green (normal colour), dark green, and olive green. These various tints are due to changes in the structure of the feathers.

Therefore, we can limit ourselves to the changes in the melanin and carotenoid. In respect of this the following main forms can be distinguished:

a. Dilute. In this mutation the amount of melanin is reduced. The colours of the Normal form remain in a lighter, diluted shade. They mainly occur as a pale grass-green. The Yellow Turquoisine is an example of this mutation;

b. Lutino-Albino-Yellow. These mutations do not produce melanin. In Lutinos and Albinos the melanine has disappeared from all external parts of the body, feathers, eyes, beak, legs, and claws; in Yellow birds this applies only to the feathers. Lutinos and Albinos are therefore always recognizable by their red eyes; normal Yellow birds do not have this. Lutinos and Albinos differ from each other in that in the Lutinos the colours yellow, orange and/or red (the carotenoid) remain; in the Albinos these have also disappeared and this results in a pure white bird with red eyes.
With regard to this it must be mentioned that when the melanine is completely absent the structural colour blue appears white;

c. Pied-Opaline. In this form melanin is absent in only parts of the plumage. As a result the Pied mutation often has a patchy and irregular plumage; the melanin often disappears from places at random, resulting in yellow or white patches. The degree to which this happens varies greatly, from only a couple of feathers to almost the entire plumage.
This mutation must not be confused with the results of certain diet deficiencies. If, for example, there is not enough of the amino acid lysine in the diet, the production of melanine can be affected. This can result in some green feathers turning yellowish while black feathers can look bleached (white). On improving the diet these feathers are replaced by normal ones during the bird's next moult. Feathers turning brown, for example on the head of a Port Lincoln, can likewise be attributed to diet.
A second mutation in this form is the so-called Opaline. In this the carotenoid becomes more intense in colour, yellow can become orange and pink red. The Opaline mutation is difficult to distinguish as the outward signs can vary in each species. I will therefore now list them with a short description of each. It concerns the Red Eastern Rosella, the Rosa Bourke's and the Pearled Cockatiel. The names given to these mutations are therefore not correct, but they have become so generally accepted that the custom is maintained here.
The entire belly and breast of the Red Eastern Rosella becomes a splendid red, and on the back a scale-like pattern of red appears.
The Rosa Bourke's is also a fine example of the Opaline mutation: the normal yellowish colours change to pure pink, the melanin disappears from the mantle, back, lesser coverts, and head. This shows a certain similarity to the Opaline Budgerigar. However, it only lacks colouring on the mantle, whereas for the Bourke's this is also on part of the wings.

The Pearled Cockatiel shows a completely different appearance: here it is from the middle of each feather that the melanin disappears, causing these to become white with a darker edge and thus forming a scaled pattern. The yellow is brighter than that of the Normal Cockatiel. The cocks lose their pearled plumage when they become adults and look almost normal. This is because they start producing more melanin then;

d. Cinnamon and Fallow. In these mutations the colour of the melanin changes: black is replaced by brown. Cinnamons are browner and Fallows are more of a brown-grey, which is especially well visible on the colour of the primaries. It should be said that cinnamon is just a nice word for beige.
These mutations show differences in appearance depending on the colour of the normal bird in question. The effect on a Cockatiel for example is very different from that on a Bourke's or Kakariki. The green becomes lighter and more yellow, and brown more brown-grey.
A reliable difference between the Cinnamon and the Fallow is that though the chicks of both are born with red eyes, those of the Cinnamons turn dark within a week and the Fallows' remain red. This means that no confusion with Yellow mutations can arise: these have dark eyes at birth. Otherwise Cinnamons and Fallows strongly resemble each other;

e. Sea Green. In these mutations the carotenoid is decreased. As a result the plumage shows less yellow, orange, and/or red. These colours do not disappear completely, only partly. In good Sea Green mutations the amount of carotenoid is decreased by half. However, they show fairly large variations. If more carotenoid disappears the colour becomes bluer, and if there is less the bird is greener. One example of this is the Sea Green Splendid;

f. Blue. If a bird becomes pure blue then no carotenoid has been produced. The yellow, orange, and red tints have therefore completely disappeared. Melanine and structural blue remain. This means that besides all the really blue birds, others, like for example the White-masked Cockatiel, fall into this category. After all, yellow and red are no longer visible in these; this mutation is not really blue because the normal colour is not green.

Forms of genetic transmission

After this short outline we go deeper into the question of how these mutations are inherited, and how the young of various combinations will turn out. To do this a few terms must first be explained; these being the four possible forms of genetic transmission and the term 'split'. The four forms are: dominant, sex-linked recessive, autosomal, and intermediate.

Dominant: if one of the birds is dominant the young will receive its colour, although it is quite possible that they will be carrying a different hidden colour. By means of certain pairings this could well appear later. The normal, wild colour is generally dominant.

Recessive: if a dominant bird is paired with a recessive one, the young will not receive the recessive parents colour as the dominant colour has priority.
The recessive bird's colour can be carried on hidden.

Sex-linked recessive: this means that the inheritance of the colour in question is linked to the sex of the birds. Therefore it is important to know which of the birds, the cock or the hen, carries the colour, as this has consequences for the colour of the young and also for their sex.

Autosomal: is derived from the term autosome. Most bird-keepers will know it is the so-called chromosomes which pass the genetic characteristics from the parent birds onto their young. One of the characteristics is the determination of sex. Some chromosomes have the power to determine sex, others do not. Autosomes are the chromosomes which pass on genetic characteristics, but do not determine sex.

Intermediate: this means that the young are somewhere between the parents with regard to colour. This form is as good as unheard of in Australian parakeets; as mentioned earlier it does appear by the so-called dark factors as light green, dark green, and olive green. If a light green bird is paired with an olive green one, the young will be dark green.

Split: it has already been mentioned that it is possible for a bird to carry a hidden colour which it can pass on to his or her young. A green bird which is carrying and can pass on blue is called a split for blue. This is often written as: green/blue.

With the help of these short explanations the following pairing possibilities will hopefully be easier to understand.
Clearly, in only one of the hereditary forms is the combination of colour and sex of importance, and that is in the sex-linked recessive: in this case a Lutino cock and a Normal hen will produce a Normal cock and a Lutino hen. In all other cases it does not make any difference to the young whether the father or the mother has the other colour.
You will not find the terms 'autosomal recessive' and 'sex-linked recessive' written full out. Instead the terms recessive and sex-linked are often used. Recessive stands for autosomal recessive, and sex-linked for sex-linked recessive.

In most cases the same mutations have the same genetic characteristics. However, there is the ocassional exception to this•rule. The Lutinos are a case in point : most inherit sex-linked recessive, but there are a few Lutino forms that inherit autosomal recessive (the Lutino Princess of Wales and the Lutino Elegant).

Tables

The majority of the mutations can be dealt with under the autosomal recessive and sex-linked recessive forms. The results of both these forms have therefore been summaried in one table; all other colours which inherit in the same way give the same results.

The colour Blue is used here as an example of *autosomal recessive inheritance*, paired with the Normal colour (Green):

parents		young	
male	female	male	female
Normal	x Blue	50% Normal/Blue	50% Normal/Blue
Blue	x Normal	50% Normal/Blue	50% Normal/Blue
Normal/Blue	x Normal	25% Normal/Blue, 25% Normal	25% Normal/Blue, 25% Normal
Normal	x Normal/Blue	25% Normal/Blue, 25% Normal	25% Normal/Blue, 25% Normal
Normal/Blue	x Blue	25% Normal/Blue, 25% Blue	25% Normal/Blue, 25% Blue
Blue	x Normal/Blue	25% Normal/Blue, 25% Blue	25% Normal/blue, 25% Blue
Normal/Blue	x Normal/Blue	25% Normal/Blue, 12.5% Normal, 12.5% Blue	25% Normal/Blue, 12.5% Normal, 12.5% Blue
Blue	x Blue	50% Blue	50% Blue

The following mutations inherit according to the same rules. They can therefore be inserted for Blue anywhere in this table:

Cockatiel	- Pied
	- Silver
	- White-masked
King Parakeet	- Yellow
Princess of Wales Parakeet	- Blue
	- Lutino
	- Albino
Barnard's Parakeet	- Blue
Pennant's Parakeet	- Blue
	- Yellow
	- White
Eastern Rosella	- Dilute
Bourke's Parakeet	- Fallow
	- Yellow
Elegant Grass Parakeet	- Lutino
Turquoisine Grass Parakeet	- Yellow
Splendid Grass Parakeet	- Yellow
	- Dilute Blue
	- White-breasted Blue

The same approach can be used for the *sex-linked recessive* form. The Rosa Bourke's is used here as an example, in combination with the Normal colour.

parents		young	
male	female	male	female
Normal	x Rosa	50% Normal/Rosa	50% Normal
Rosa	x Normal	50% Normal/Rosa	50% Rosa
Normal/Rosa	x Normal	25% Normal, 25% Normal/Rosa	25% Normal, 25% Rosa
Normal/Rosa	x Rosa	25% Normal/Rosa, 25% Rosa	25% Normal, 25% Rosa
Rosa	x Rosa	50% Rosa	25% Rosa

Here too applies that the following mutations all inherit according to the same rules. Rosa can therefore be replaced by any of them:

Cockatiel	- Pearled
	- Cinnamon
	- Lutino
	- Albino
Red-rumped Parakeet	- Yellow (Cinnamon)
Red-fronted Kakariki	- Cinnamon
Bourke's Parakeet	- Cinnamon
Splendid Grass Parakeet	- Cinnamon

So far we have only been concerned with pairing one colour with a Normal (split or non-split) bird.

The next step is to cross mutations. This is where it gets a bit more complicated, but even then everything can be reduced to a couple of tables. In order to do that we have to make combinations of both the (autosomal) recessive and the sex-linked (recessive) forms. There are four possibilities:
sex-linked x sex-linked
sex-linked x recessive
recessive x sex-linked
recessive x recessive.

There follows an example of each of these combinations. If you want to know what result you can expect from a particular crossing, first look which genetic rules apply for both birds. Then you look to see into which of the following tables this fits, and simply replace the colours which are given by the ones you want to bring together. Then simply read off the result:

| parents | | young |
male	female	
sex-linked Lutino Cockatiel	x sex-linked x Pearled Cockatiel	males : 50% Normal/Lutino/Pearled females : 50% Lutino
sex-linked Lutino Cockatiel	x recessive x Pied Cockatiel	males : 50% Normal/Lutino/Pied females : 50% Lutino/Pied
recessive Pied Cockatiel	x sex-linked x Pearled Cockatiel	males : 50% Normal/Pied/Pearled females : 50% Normal/Pied
recessive Yellow Pennant's	x recessive x Blue Pennant's	males : 50% Normal/Yellow/Blue females : 50% Normal/Yellow/Blue

Everyone that has been able to follow this so far will have realised that we are now dealing with birds that are split for two colours.
From the first combination of Lutino x Pearled Cockatiel come only Normal coloured cocks that are split for both Lutino and Pearled.
If in this table the Lutino Cockatiel is replaced by a Cinnamon, you get 50% Normal/Cinnamon/Pearled cocks and 50% Cinnamon hens, etc.

Finally a couple of comments about the breeding of Albino mutations. There is a chance that you will find these in your clutches if you possess Blue and Lutino birds and arrange the correct crossing. The best pairing to begin with is a sex-linked Lutino cock with a recessive Blue hen. The reverse is however also possible. These combinations give the following results:

| parents | | young | |
male	female	male	female
Lutino Blue	x Blue x Lutino	50% Normal/Lutino/Blue 50% Normal/Lutino/Blue	50% Lutino/Blue 50% Normal/Blue

Using the young there are a number of combinations possible to breed Albinos:

parents		young	
male	female		
Normal/Lutino/Blue	x Blue	male	: 12.5% Normal/Blue, 12.5% Blue, 12.5% Normal/Lutino/Blue, 12.5% Blue/Albino
		female	: 12.5% Normal/Blue, 12.5% Blue, 12.5% Lutino/Blue, 12.5% Albino
Normal/Lutino/Blue	x Lutino/Blue	male	: 6.25% Normal/Lutino, 6.25% Lutino, 12.5% Normal/Lutino/Blue, 12.5% Lutino/Blue, 6.25% Albino, 6.25% Blue/Albino
		female	: 6.25% Normal, 12.5% Normal/Blue, 6.25% Lutino, 12.5% Lutino/Blue, 6.25% Blue, 6.25% Albino
Normal/Lutino/Blue	x Normal/Blue	male	: 12.5% Normal/Blue, 6.25% Normal, 12.5% Normal/Lutino/Blue, 6.25% Normal/Lutino, 6.25% Blue, 6.25% Blue/Lutino
		female	: 12.5% Normal/Blue, 6.25% Normal, 12.5% Lutino/Blue, 6.25% Lutino, 6.25% Blue, 6.25% Albino

Two important points are relevant to everything that has been dealt with in this chapter. The first is that all the percentages given by the results are averages; not every clutch will consist of exactly 50% cocks and 50% hens. Secondly, these tables are only correct if it is known exactly which genetic rules apply to the parents and which colours they are carrying. If something else comes out of a combination than could be expected from what is stated here, then at least one of the parents is carrying a hidden colour which is unknown to the breeder.

Colour changes also occur in parakeets which cannot be considered as real mutations. These are often the result of the selective breeding of birds which already have abnormalities in the plumage. As a case in point one might think of the Red-bellied Turquoisine and the Red-bellied Splendid. These have developed from birds which already had a relatively large amount of red; this becomes accentuated by selective breeding and exceptionally fine birds can result. Therefore it is always important to take care when choosing birds for mating.

Clearly there can be no question of a sudden colour change occurring; the ultimate result is only reached step by step.

VIII. Diseases and disorders

Sick birds do not represent the most pleasant aspect of the hobby, but it is something that just cannot be avoided. Every bird-keeper will be confronted with illness and therefore some knowledge of the prevention and treatment of it should be gained. It is nearly always much easier to see that a bird is ill than it is to establish what is wrong with it. Therefore, there is no point in dealing with all the possible diseases here. For one thing, I am not sufficiently knowledgeable on the subject, and for another, it would be of little use to the average reader, as he only has the outward signs of the disease to go on; and the clinical picture often gives few indications for the correct diagnosis of the ailment.

In most cases the fact that a bird is ill can be seen from the following symptoms:

a. it sits hunched up on the perch and has little or no interest in what is going on around. After a fairly short time it stops going to the food container, which speeds up the progress of the illness even more;

b. the bird sits with closed eyes and its head tucked under its back feathers, and both feet on the perch. When its eyes are open they look lacklustre;

c. the feathers do not lie smooth along the body but have an untidy appearance;

d. the droppings usually have a different colour and consistency than is normal. The droppings of a bird normally consist of two ingredients: the white, watery part is urine, the rest varies from black or brown to greenish depending partly on the bird's diet. Sick birds often have thin droppings and the colour can change to, for example, yellow; the white is then no longer visible.

What attitude should an aviculturist have towards diseases? In the first place his basic care should be aimed at their prevention. The conditions for this are good hygiene and a well-balanced diet, which allows the birds to build up the necessary resistance. Moreover, it is advisable to supply some protection against bad weather, paying particular attention to damp, draughts, and the cold. However, such measures will not prevent the occasional bird falling ill. The important thing then is to take steps immediately, as the process works incredibly quickly; twelve hours later is sometimes already too late.

It is therefore important for you to be constantly on the alert. Make a rule of visiting all your birds at least twice a day; develop the habit of automatically glancing at each bird as you walk past the aviaries. It costs only little effort and it can save you a lot of suffering.

Do not waste a moment if you find a sick bird but take immediate action. First you must decide which course to take: treat it yourself or call in the vet. The most obvious would seem to be to consult a vet. Unfortunately, after years of experience I have to say that, for some reason or other, many of them do not seem to be able to accurately diagnose the disease they are looking at. After talking to various bird-keepers it appears that I certainly do not stand alone in my opinion.

Therefore, go preferably to a vet who is specialised and interested in birds. Unfortunately for us parakeet enthusiasts they are few and far between. However, we can improve the situation by pooling our experiences with vets, and then by getting all the people living in one region to go to just one of them, so that he gets the opportunity to gain experience in the treatment of parakeets and parrots. If you do not know of such a vet, ask your fellow enthusiasts.

If you decide to nurse the patient yourself, there are three or four basic treatments which are of importance: warmth, a widely applicable antibiotic, vitamins and trace elements, and a dewormer.

Warmth

You can supply warmth in two ways: in a hospital cage or by means of an infra-red lamp. Hospital cages can be bought ready made or you can make them yourself. The size should be such that your biggest bird will fit in it; the minimum sizes are 45cm (18in) high, 35cm (14in) wide, and 25cm (10in) deep. It must contain a heat source which is controlled by a thermostat, and can produce a temperature of at least 30°C.

Every light bulb is a source of heat, but their disadvantage is that they also produce light. It is very disturbing for the bird if the thermostat turns the lamp, and consequently also the light, on and off when the required temperature has been reached. Therefore, it is much better to use an infra-red lamp, which produces heat but no light (which must then be arranged some other way).

If lamps are fitted under the cage, you must make sure that no droppings can fall onto them. It is better to attach the lamps - protected by wire mesh - to one of the sides.

A very ill bird will remain on the floor of the cage, but as it gets better it will go back to sitting on a perch. Particularly for the larger species, such a cage is too small to fly in, so make sure that there is another way in which the patient can reach the perch; by fitting a ladder for example.

The containers for food and water can be placed on the floor. See to it that the drinking water is changed regularly; after all, the temperature is high, and if any medicine has been added to the water it goes bad very quickly. When giving medicine in the water do not supply any food containing a lot of liquid, as this will reduce the bird's need to drink.

A drawback of a hospital cage is that the air in it is very dry, and if the hygiene is not perfect it becomes dusty; which is not good for the bird. A solution for this is to make one side, for example the front, of glass and wire mesh in such a way that the glass can be slid out to let in fresh air.

After a sick bird has been placed into the cage, the temperature must be increased to at least 30°C. As the patient gets better the temperature can be decreased until the bird is able to convalesce outside the cage. Make sure that the reintroduction to the outside world is gradual.

The second alternative is to fix an infra-red lamp onto the outside of a wire cage. A perch must then be placed along the line of the lamp, so that the bird can choose the most suitable temperature by sitting further away from or closer to it. With this arrangement the air is less dry and the bird can remain in the cage until it is fully recovered. Place the lamp between ten and twenty centimetres from the cage. You can tell by the bird's behaviour if it is too hot or too cold. If necessary you can then reposition the lamp. This arrangement is much simpler and no thermostat is needed. However, the lamp must be kept burning day and night.

Antibiotics

A bird falling ill suddenly should be placed in a hospital cage, after which the patient can be treated with antibiotics. Antibiotics are the means to kill bacteria (anti = against, bios = life). There are also means effective against e.g. fungi (antimyotics). Which means would be most effective in which situation is usually hard to decide without a laboratory research.

Some important antibiotics used in bird medicine are Chloramphenicol, Oxytetracyclin and Doxycyclin.
The major fungal diseases are aspergillosis and candidiasis. Fungi can be treated by e.g. Nystatin and Ketaconazole.
It is only possible to buy these medicines from or through a vet. They are not given just once, but in a course lasting a number of days. This is always stated on each type.

In order to rebuild the sick bird's resistance as rapidly as possible it should not only be given supplementary foodstuffs, but extra vitamins, minerals and trace elements should be provided as well.

Worms

It is also possible that an unwell bird is infested with worms. This is difficult to tell by its behaviour as the symptoms are the same as those already mentioned.
Generally speaking worm infestations need no longer be a problem. The treatment of worms is one of the most basic aspects of the hobby, and there are good preparations on the market. An excellent one is Fenbendazol; the prescribed dosage of this white liquid can be given to each bird using a dropper. It is available from pet shops specializing in birds. Preparations such as Ripercol are sometimes recommended; these are effective enough, but a drawback is that they kill the worms very quickly and then these sometimes have to be passed all in one go. This can cause obstructions in the intestines which can result in the bird's death. In this respect Fenbendazol works more slowly; it takes a couple of days for all the worms to pass through the body.

At present Fenbendazol (Panacur 2.5) is available in ready-made solutions (dosage: 1ml per kilo bodyweight). It will keep for about three years. It should be administered either by way of a dropper or a crop needle, whereas Ripercol is mixed into the bird's drinking water.

Another possibility is to make a preparation yourself. For a couple of pence you can make a comparable preparation which would otherwise cost twenty times as much or more. The basic ingredient is Panacur, the active ingredient of which is the above mentioned Fenbendazol. Panacur is available from your vet.

You take 5g of Panacur and add red grenadine until you have 20cc of liquid. 1g of Panacur is a level small teaspoonful. This 20cc is enough for 400 drops, so 1cc contains 20 drops. The preparation must be shaken well before and during use, as the Panacur powder tends to sink. The only disadvantage with this preparation is that it can only be kept for a couple of months, as then it starts to ferment. However, this is not too much of a problem; you can make the amounts required and then throw away any that is left over. The Panacur powder can be kept for at least two years.

Once you have prepared a mixture in the above mentioned way, you can work out for yourself how much your birds need in the following manner:
1g of Panacur contains 0.04g = 40mg of Fenbendazol. As a rule you can say that parakeets must have on average 25mg of Fenbendazol for every kilo of bodyweight. Smaller birds can have a little more; with Neophemas you can go up to 40mg without any problem.
On the basis of 25mg for every kilo, you will need two drops of the mixture for a bird weighing 40g. For a bird of 80g, 4 drops, for one of 120g, 6 drops, and so on.

It is not strictly necessary for you to know how this is worked out, but for anybody who is interested I will nevertheless show how it is done.

The mixture contains 5g of Panacur, and thus 5 x 0.04g = 0.2g of Fenbendazol. This 0.2g is divided over 400 drops, which means that one drop contains 0.5mg of Fenbendazol. 25mg of Fenbendazol is needed for a bird weighing 1000g; 1mg, or two drops, is therefore enough for a 40g bird.

The weight of each (sub)species is given in chapter IX; using these it is easy to work out the number of drops. A slight overdose is not harmful. For the sake of convenience there follows the amounts necessary for a number of species:

Bourke's, Turquoisine	2-3 drops
Many-coloured Parakeet	3 drops
Cockatiel	4 drops
Eastern Rosella, Barnard's	6 drops
Pennant's	7 drops
Rock Pebbler	8 drops
King	12 drops

Specific disorders

After these general comments, something can be said about a few more specific disorders which will be clearly recognizable to every bird-keeper.

Firstly egg-binding, which is a condition whereby the hen is unable to lay her egg. This is not very common, but everyone will encounter it at some time. The hen sits hunched on her perch, or, if it gets worse, on the floor and appears to be suffering from cramp. This is due to the muscle action of the body trying to force out the egg. In such cases the most important medicine is warmth. Place the bird in a temperature of at least 30°C and give her plenty of time, because it is not true that the egg will be laid within half an hour; it can really take quite a time. In addition, a few drops of salad oil is sometimes put on to the cloaca, in the hope that this will help the egg to slide out more easily. In most cases this disorder arises with the first egg only, and once this has been laid there are usually no more problems.

Feather plucking can be a very troublesome habit. It is true that the bird is not ill, but you should still try and put a stop to it, otherwise the bird will not be well enough protected against the cold in the autumn and winter.
In order to do something about it, it is important to discover the cause, although this is often easier said than done. It can be due to a deficiency in the diet, but it is more likely to be either a psychological problem or a question of boredom. Have a look into matters such as diet, housing, pairing, and distractions. The diet must contain everything the bird needs; if you feed your birds a couple of times a day, they will spend more time eating and will have less time for other activities.

The accomodation must be big enough for the bird to be able to fly around in and entertain itself. A bird should not sit on its own, but with a suitable partner that it can get on with. Together, all these matters can supply the necessary distraction, and things can be improved still further by giving the birds something to do: give them a varied diet, regular fresh twigs, rotten pieces of wood which might contain insects. Sometimes removing the birds to another aviary can be the solution.

Sometimes one or both of the parents are found to be plucking their young. The removal of the lid of the nest-box, whereby the inside of the box becomes much lighter, has been known to put a stop to this. Sometimes it also helps to remove the cock temporarily. Finally, the chicks can be removed from the box and placed on the floor of the shelter. The parents will carrying on feeding and the plucking often stops.

Eye infections occasionally affect birds, particularly those of the Polytelis species. This can be transmitted to other birds. Parakeets which are suffering from it like to wipe their eyes on the perches and so infect others. It is therefore important to keep everything extra clean, and to put the bird in question alone. Vets often prescribe an antibiotic cream, which has to be rubbed into the eye regularly.

I came across a story in an Australian magazine from someone who had ten Rock Pebblers with this infection. They all received an injection of Tylan 50 (Tylan is the brand name of the antibiotic Tylosine) in the breast muscle. After only two days there were clear signs of improvement. After three days these were even clearer, and after eight days' treatment seven of the ten were completely cured. The other three birds were then given five days' rest and then treated again. By the end of the second course, two of the three were cured of the infection. The third was probably resistant to the drug as it had the infection for over a year.

Australian parakeets do not often show signs of the effects of frostbite as they are not very susceptible to it. However, if it does occur, the first places to be affected are the legs and claws. Therefore, it is advisable to make the perches so big that the birds can let their bodies fall right over their toes; this way t03hey are less exposed to the cold.
It is possible to spot if claws and/or toes are frostbitten when the bird keeps its leg tucked up and does not stand on it. If you do not act in time, the claws will fall out, and even part of the toes can disappear and perhaps start bleeding. This can be stopped with iron chloride.

As soon as you notice that a bird is suffering from frostbite, catch it and place it in a frost free place. Bear in mind that it must not be too warm! Many inexperienced enthusiasts are inclined to put such parakeets somewhere nice and warm, but that is the worst thing you can do.

Claws and toes which have been frozen off do not regrow. Once the wounds have healed the birds will no longer be troubled by them. However, they do generally become more sensitive to frost, so you must be extra attentive in subsequent winters.

One or more missing claws is not a handicap as far as mating is concerned; they manage to do this regardless. There are even stories of cocks with only one leg who manage to produce offspring.

Advice and requirements

If you have a sick bird, ultimately you must decide what to do with it yourself. If you take it to a vet, take it to one that you know, or have heard about, who is expert in the field of birds, and parakeets in particular.

If there is not one in your area, or should you decide to treat the bird yourself, make sure that you always have the following in stock at home:
-   a hospital cage or a mesh cage with an infra-red lamp;
-   a widely applicable antibiotic, e.g. Vibramycine or Lutricycline;
-   a dewormer, e.g. Fenbendazol or Panacur;
-   a haemostatic (blood-clotting) agent, e.g. iron chloride;
-   a disinfectant, e.g. Halamid;
-   a preparation against parasites such as blood and feather mites;
-   a dropper or a crop needle to administer medicine.

If you do not know where exactly to obtain these articles, consult an experienced aviculturist. There will almost certainly be one living somewhere near, and you should feel free to get in touch. After years of experience such a person will know what to do with a sick bird. Very often they will be able to help you better than a vet who is chiefly concerned with farm animals and domestic cats and dogs.

If the sick bird fails to recover and dies, you have a choice of three things which you can do with it:
a.   put it in the dustbin. Unfortunately this is where the majority end up immediately;
b.   have the bird examined by an expert. This way you at least get to know what was wrong with the bird, and you might be able to use this knowledge to your advantage in a subsequent case;
c.   open up the bird yourself and see how the patient looks on the inside, and see if you can find anything unusual. You could possibly do this with the help of an experienced aviculturist. This is the most advisable thing to do, because you can learn such a lot from it. Even if it is only to find out where the genital organs are and what they look like; if you had any doubts concerning the bird's sex, you can clear them up this way.

Finally: if you intend to treat sick birds occasionally, buy one or two books on the subject. There are a number of good ones on the market which give the necessary information. However, you must be conscious of the fact that in most cases it will remain difficult, if not impossible for you, as a layman, to exactly identify the problem.

IX. Species descriptions

In this chapter a systematic description is given of the thirteen genuses and the thirty-nine (sub)species of parakeets. Eleven of the genuses can be found at least partly on the Australian continent, one in New Zealand or on the surrounding islands, and one in New Caledonia. There are also species which come under the first eleven which inhabit the Indonesian islands, New Guinea, and Tasmania.

What exactly are genuses and what is species? A genus can comprise of one species (for example the cockatiel) or a number of species (for example the Rosellas), and forms a distinct group of birds which have a shared origin and common characteristics which clearly distinguishes them from other groups.
Classification is not only based on appearance, but also on build, the construction of the skeleton, etc.
A species is described as a group of birds which reproduces within that group, and thus do not mate with birds of other species.
Some species can be split again into subspecies. These are groups of birds that often differ only very slightly from each other and only reproduce within the group; they do not pair with other subspecies because in the wild they live in different areas and, therefore, do not meet each other. If this should happen, crossbreeding would certainly take place. For a number of subspecies this is indeed the case, and their range of distribution is often very great.
Subspecies from the centres of their range are clearly distinguishable, but towards the edges where ranges overlap we find hybrids, and it is often difficult to see to which subspecies such birds belong.

The division into genus, species, and subspecies or races is universally known and applied. However, in practice it transpires that there are differences of opinion about the classification of certain birds, especially when deciding if they are a species or sub-species. Examples of this are the Rock Pebbler, the Adelaide Rosella and the Bourke's. I do mention this in the descriptions, though a general agreement will never be reached on this point as such minimal differences are concerned.

Every bird has a scientific Latin name, consisting of two or three words. This makes it possible for people throughout the world to use the same name for the same bird. The use of national names occasionally leads to misunderstandings. The scientific name of the Golden-mantled Rosella is *Platycercus eximius cecilae* Mathews. *Platycercus* is the name of the genus, *eximius* that of the species, and *cecilae* that of the subspecies. After that comes the name of the person who described and named the bird; in this case a certain Mr Mathews. This name is sometimes put between brackets. If this is the case it means that the bird was placed in a different genus in the original description.

Sometimes subspecies differ from each other because they live in different climatic zones. A couple of general rules apply here which are known as Bergmann's Law and Gloger's Law.

Bergmann's Law states that subspecies which come from warmer climates are smaller. Birds from colder climates are bigger: they have a smaller body surface area in relation to their weight and, therefore, they are less susceptible to undercooling. Smaller birds weigh less but have a relatively large body surface area, but as they live in warmer areas this is not a problem. An example is the Pennant's Parakeet, whose subspecies *Platycercus elegans nigrescens* lives in a warmer area and is smaller than the normal Pennant's *Platycercus elegans elegans*. Another example, nearer to home, is our bullfinch, which is smaller than the bullfinch found in the relatively cold Scandinavian regions.

Gloger's Law states that subspecies from wet areas produce more melanine, and therefore are darker in colour, than subspecies from drier climatic zones. Here too the Pennant's Parakeet can be taken as an example; the subspecies *Platycercus elegans nigrescens* lives in a wetter area and is darker. Reference is occasionally made to these laws in the text.

An attempt has been made to keep the contents of this chapter orderly and concise. The texts and photographs have been placed next to each other as far as possible. A photogragh of every species and of several subspecies has been included, which means that it has not been necessary to give a detailed description of the plumage. Now and then specific points have been mentioned when possible.
The more general aspects such as accommodation, diet, and breeding have already been dealt with in separate chapters, so they do not need to be extensively dealt with here. If you wish to learn about a particular species, it is a good idea to read through the information on the other species belonging to the same genus, as related species often have much in common.
Photographs have not been included of all the existing mutations. In the first place, it was not possible because they are not (yet) all to be found in Holland, and in the second place, it is the intention of this book only to give a rough idea of the possibilities that exist in this field.

The particulars given about incubation and fledging times and so forth may, in practice, sometimes appear slightly incorrect. As such matters are dependent on varying circumstances, it is only possible to give averages. You will often be unable to ascertain exactly when the hen has started incubating. Furthermore, aspects such as climate and diet are also a great influence. If it is cold, the incubation time could be longer, and if it is warm, a little shorter. Therefore, take these factors into account.

Genus *Nymphicus*

Only one species belongs to this genus, namely the Cockatiel. It is regarded as an intermediate form between the cockatoos and the parakeets, of which especially the great similarity to the appearance and behaviour of the cockatoos is striking. For this reason this genus is usually placed under the cockatoos:
-    the Cockatiel has a crest, although it is not able to raise it;
-    the hens have bars on the underside of their tails;
-    both the hen and the cock incubate;
-    the cock does not feed the hen: this is not necessary as both parents feed and care for the chicks after they have hatched;
-    the colour grey is hardly ever found in Cockatiels, but it is found in cockatoos;
-    the patches on the cheeks are similar to those of some cockatoos;
-    when drinking, the birds make a scooping movement with their beaks, and then the head is held over backwards;
-    when excited or angry they produce a hissing noise.

genus	species	subspecies	
Nymphicus	*hollandicus*	-	Cockatiel

COCKATIEL - *Nymphicus hollandicus*

Subspecies
None.

Origin of name
Nymphicus: nymph-like.
Hollandicus: from (New-)Holland, an earlier name for Australia.
Dutch: valkparkiet.
German: Nymphensittich.

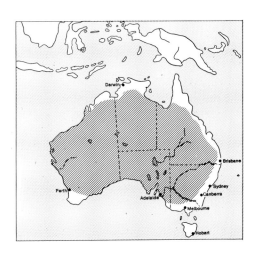

Parents and young
The underside of the tail of the hen is barred, whereas that of the cock is an almost uniform grey. The head of the hen is for the most part grey; the red and yellow is much less bright than in the cock. Sex determination of young birds is not always as simple as it might be. Young birds look similar to the hen, but they often have shorter tails. Cocks can be identified with varying ease by the following characteristics: they may have more yellow or orange on their heads, after three months they start to 'sing', and the edges of the outside tail feathers are grey, and not yellowish-white like those of hens. After the first moult, at an age of five or six months, the colours on the head make the difference much more obvious; although the stripes on the tail remain visible until the cock is almost a year old. Only then is it full-grown, fully fledged, and sexually mature.

Sizes and weights
Length: 32cm (13in)
Weights: cock 80-102g, hen 89-92g.
Ring size: 5.4mm.

Habitat and habits
The Cockatiel is found in most types of open country almost throughout the whole of Australia, but seldom far from water.
It does not remain in one region; with the exception of the budgerigar it is the bird which travels round the most. Its movements are determined by the availability of food and water. The influence of this is stronger in the north of the continent than in the south: there the movements are related more to the seasons.
In the wild this parakeet is usually found in groups of between two and twelve; though sometimes flocks of as many as several hundred birds are formed. They spend a lot of time on the ground searching for food, as they are almost entirely dependent on the seeds of grasses and bushes.

6. *Cockatiel, female and male*

They drink in the morning and evening, and these birds like to stand in the water while drinking. During the day they often sit lengthwise on (dead) branches resting; this camouflages them well. This behaviour can also be observed in the aviary.

The Cockatiel is widespread and common in the wild; it is the fastest flyer of all the Australian parrot-likes. Although they are fairly shy they adjust to aviaries fairly easily.

Diet

The menu consists mainly of the seeds of grasses, bushes, and trees, and for the rest of cereals, berries and other wild fruits, blossom, nectar, and insects. They have a preference for acacia seeds, which are eaten in the bush or sitting on the ground under it.

Compared to other parakeets they eat large quantities.

Nest-site

The cock first chooses a nest-site and then the hen arrives to inspect it. She does not always agree with her mate's choice, and in that case the process is repeated with a second hole. Incidentally, this occurs more often in the wild than in aviaries, as, after many years in captivity, the Cockatiel has adjusted to them and has become a bit less choosy.

In the wild, nests are found in both large open holes, and in small narrow niches; sometimes they are vertical, sometimes horizontal, sometimes only one metre (3ft) above the ground, and sometimes as much as ten (30ft). They are far from all closed at the top. A number of nests are sometimes found in one tree.

In the aviary the nest box does not need to be bigger than 30 x 18 x 18cm (12 x 7 x 7in); a diameter of 6cm (2½in) is sufficient for the entrance hole.

Breeding process

A clutch numbers four to seven eggs, which are incubated for about nineteen days. The first is usually laid ten to fourteen days after the first mating.

Both the hen and the cock incubate, just like cockatoos. The cock sits from the early morning to the late afternoon, when he is relieved by the hen. They sit extremely tight and are not easily disturbed.

Both parents feed the chicks from the moment they hatch. The chicks' eyes open after about eight days. They can be ringed between the sixth and the tenth day, depending on their rate of growth. When the chicks are about thirty-five days old they leave the nest-box. For the first few days they are very shy and nervous.

Cockatiels in captivity have more and more the tendency to rear one clutch after the other. If this is the case, it is advisable to remove the nest-box. They should not be allowed to have more than three clutches in one season. After the third clutch it is a good idea to keep an eye on the nest, because eggs are sometimes laid again even before the chicks have left the nest-box. Should this happen, wait in any case until the clutch is complete before removing them.

It is possible to breed Cockatiels in colonies. Some aviculturists get better results if three or four pairs are kept together. It is advisable to release all the birds into the aviary at the same time; the aviary must be sufficiently large, there must be more nest-boxes than pairs of birds, and the number of cocks and hens must be the same.

7. Cockatiel, Albino and Silver-Pearl

General remarks

Cockatiels can live to an age of twenty-five. Hens can still be laying after twenty years, but the eggs are not always fertile.

They are ideal birds for someone who is just starting: they are hardy, are easy to breed, and they are not aggressive. Moreover, more and more mutations are appearing, which makes breeding more attractive.

Chicks in the nest-box produce unusually large quantities of droppings, so it is important to put in some form of material that soaks up moisture. This must not be too fine, as the chicks could develop breathing problems as a result of the dust.

Finally, a Cockatiel can give a lot of pleasure as a pet. If a bird is removed from the nest-box just before it fledges and then fed by hand, it can be favourably compared to the average Amazon or African Grey. They become very tame and affectionate. The only thing is that it will not learn to talk, this being the case in some of the parrots.

Mutations

Over the years various mutations and combinations of mutations have appeared. At one time such birds were extremely expensive, however, as this species breeds so freely, it only takes a couple of years until they are within the means of the average birdkeeper.

The most important mutations produced so far are: Pied, Pearl, Cinnamon, Silver, White-faced, Lutino, and Albino.

Pied: the plumage is covered in irregular white spots or patches. The pattern is exceptionally variable; from only a few white feathers to almost completely white. A fine overall effect is reached when both sides of the bird have the same pattern, but this is almost impossible to achieve. The mode of inheritance is autosomal recessive.

Pearl: in Budgerigars this mutation is called Opaline. The feathers on the neck, mantle, and wings have white centres and dark grey edges; this produces a scale-like pattern. As the cocks become mature they lose this pattern during the moult; they are then difficult to distinguish from a normal cock. The pearled pattern varies somewhat, and young birds from the same clutch are rarely exactly alike. The mode of inheritance is sex-linked recessive.

Cinnamon (also called Isabel): the feathers are a brownish-grey; the colour of cinnamon. Newly-hatched chicks have red eyes; however, these turn dark before they are a week old. The mode of inheritance is autosomal recessive.

White-faced: this mutation lacks the colours yellow and red and in this respect it is similar to a Blue Princess of Wales Parakeet or any other standard blue mutation. The mode of inheritance is therefore the same as them: autosomal recessive.

Lutino: disagreement about the correctness of this name sometimes causes misunderstandings. This bird is fairly generally known as the White Cockatiel. Indeed, the bird makes a white impression, but it is only the black-grey tints which have disappeared; the yellow and red remain. The amount of yellow is very variable; ranging from the head, to a yellow sheen over the whole plumage. The characteristics of this Lutino is the same as a number of other lutino mutations: sex-linked recessive.

Albino: this is the truly white Cockatiel; no other colours are visible. Albinos can be bred from a combination of the intermediate forms Lutino x White-faced. The Albino has red eyes the same as the Lutino, and the mode of inheritance is sex-linked recessive.

Various intermediate forms are possible from combinations of these mutations. For example, a Pied can be crossed with a Cinnamon, Pearl, or Silver; or Cinnamon with Silver; or Pearl with Lutino. Certain colours (for example Silver and Cinnamon) can theoretically be bred into any other colour. However, there is not always any point, as the colour change is not always visible (among others by a combination of Lutino and Albino).

8. Cockatiel: Pearl, Cinnamon,
and Lutino

Genus *Alisterus*

This genus comprises of three species and eleven subspecies. They are robust birds with a mainly red and green plumage. They spend most of their time in trees, but they do come down to the ground to drink.

King Parakeets are found in eastern Australia and also on a number of the New Guinea islands as far as the Moluccas. The hens are generally dominant.

There is little difference between the cock and hen of all the subspecies of the Amboina King Parakeet; this is also true of number 5. The difference is very clear in numbers 1 to 4 inclusive. The young of these all resemble the hen, whereas the young of the Amboina have a juvenile plumage.

It is striking that where, in the wild, the range of the King Parakeet overlaps that of the Crimson-winged Parakeet (numbers 1, 2 and 3), the cock and hen are different; but where this is not the case (numbers 4 to 11 inclusive), both sexes are almost alike.

The same goes for the Crimson-winged Parakeet: where they overlap the King Parakeet (in Australia), the cock and hen differ, and where they do not overlap, they look much more alike: This is also true for the Timor Crimson-winged Parakeet, which is found on the Indonesian islands of Timor and Wetar.

genus	species	subspecies	
Alisterus	*scapularis*	*scapularis*	1. Australian King Parakeet
"	"	*minor*	2. (Lesser) King Parakeet
"	*chloropterus*	*chloropterus*	3. Green-winged King Parakeet
"	"	*callopterus*	4. Fly River King Parakeet
"	"	*moszkowskii*	5. Moszkowski King Parakeet
"	*amboinensis*	*amboinensis*	6. Amboina King Parakeet
"	"	*sulaensis*	7. Sula King Parakeet
"	"	*versicolor*	8. Peleng King Parakeet
"	"	*buruensis*	9. Buru King Parakeet
"	"	*hypophonius*	10. Halmahera King Parakeet
"	"	*dorsalis*	11. Salawati King Parakeet

9. *Australian King Parakeet; the light green wing bar of the cock is not clearly visible*

KING PARAKEET - *Alisterus scapularis*

Subspecies

1. *Alisterus scapularis scapularis*
                    Australian King Parakeet
2. *Alisterus scapularis minor*
                    (Lesser) King Parakeet

The only difference between the two is that the second is a little smaller. In captivity they are almost impossible to tell apart, as a result of cross-breeding.

Origin of name

Alisterus: this genus was named by Gregory M. Mathews, who named it after his son Alister.
Scapularis: shouldered.
Minor: smaller.
Dutch: koningsparkiet.
German: Königssittich.

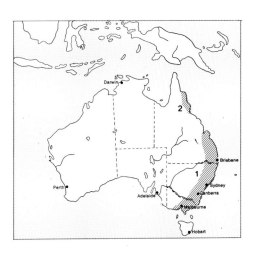

Parents and young

Adult cocks develop red breasts, throats and heads, whereas those of the hen remain green. The cock also has a light green wing bar and a red upper mandible. Very occasionally a light green bar is also faintly visible on the wings of the hen.

When they fledge, the young birds closely resemble the hen. The beak of the young hen is sometimes a little darker than that of the cock. Immature cocks already show signs of the wing bar, and the red on the belly often stretches a little higher. The rump of the immature cock is dark blue, and that of the hen a brighter and lighter blue.

Cocks begin to get their adult plumage within a year: red feathers start appearing here and there on the head and/or breast, while the beak also gradually turns red. I saw red feathers already appearing on one of my young birds in October, at an age of about six months. This colour change happens very slowly, and goes on for the two and a half years that it approximately takes the bird to develop its adult plumage.

In the wild King Parakeets become sexually mature at about the beginning of their third year. In captivity hens will sometimes rear young in their second year, and very occasionally they will even breed when they are only one year old. Cocks must be at least two, and usually three, years old before they are able to fertilize the eggs.

Sizes and weights

Length: 43cm (17in).
Weights: cock 209-227g, hen 220-275g.
Ring size: 7mm.

Habitat and habits

The King Parakeet is a common bird in the coastal plains and mountainous regions of eastern Australia, up to an altitude of 2000 metres (6500ft). It is a woodland bird by nature and lives in the lower branches in (eucalyptus) woods and subtropical rainforests. However, it can also regularly be seen in the more open, lightly-wooded areas bordering them, and also in fields of cereals and orchards. Although this bird lives in trees, it comes down to the ground to eat and drink. Particularly during the breeding season it appears in the parks and gardens of towns and villages in fairly large numbers, and is then very tame.

King Parakeets usually fly around in pairs or in small groups. In autumn the young birds come together in small flocks of twenty or thirty. Most of the day is spent searching for food, and resting in trees and bushes.

They are strong fliers but are not as noisy and active as most other Australian parakeets.

10. Australian King Parakeet; this cock is eighteen months old

Diet

In the wild their diet consists of berries and other wild fruit, nuts, seeds of grass and other plants, bushes and trees, nectar, blossom and buds, and also insects and their larvae. They have a preference for the seeds of eucalyptuses and acacias, and for half ripe maize. Birds in captivity require a varied menu, with lots of fruit, berries and green food.

Nest-site

In the wild the nest is usually made in the trunk of a tall tree in a wood. The nest is usually deep in the tree, whereby the eggs can end up almost at ground level. Cases have been recorded in which the entrance hole was 10 metres (30ft) above ground, while the eggs were less than one metre (3ft) above ground level.

In captivity King Parakeets are fairly particular in their choice of nest-site. This can lead to the hens either not laying at all, or releasing their eggs while sitting on the perch, or in some cases even laying their eggs on the ground.

They generally prefer a standing nest-box measuring 180 to 200cm (5ft 11ins to 6ft 7in) tall and a floor surface area of 25 x 25cm (10 x 10in). They prefer to breed in an outside flight and at ground level, in a dark, cool spot. I came across a case in which a hen laid on the ground even though there was a nest box measuring 60 x 23 x 25cm available, she still did not show any interest when she was supplied with a box measuring 60 x 23 x

25cm; only when a box measuring 180 x 23 x 25cm arrived was she tempted. However, young have been reared in hanging nest boxes with depths of 60-100cm (2ft - 3ft 3in). The young cock in the photograph was born in a 50 x 30 x 30cm chipboard box, with a 9cm (3.5in) diameter entrance hole.

Breeding process

A clutch numbers three to six eggs, which the hen incubates for about twenty days. The cock remains in the vicinity and feeds her regularly. When the chicks are a few days old he also helps to feed them. They fledge after about thirty-five days; in the wild they then remain with the parents for several more weeks. After some time they form goups of twenty to thirty with other immature birds.

General remarks

King Parakeets are not very suitable for the inexperienced birdkeeper. They are not very easy to breed and they are particular when it comes to choosing a mate and a nest site. They are not aggressive and can be tamed if the necessary effort is put into it.
They are hardy and can withstand low temperatures. Baths are taken in the rain, and not in standing water.
The flight must be at least 5 metres (16ft 6in) long. They are not shown to their advantage if the flight is too short and they can become lethargic and inactive.
As they are woodland birds by nature, bare aviaries are not very suitable; the lack of cover possibly makes them feel ill at ease, and this could be one of the reasons why breeding is often unsuccessful. Enthusiasts who wish to obtain this species would be well advised to buy young birds, place them together immediately and after that not to make any changes. They should be supplied with a number of nest-boxes to choose from.

Mutations

A Yellow mutation (not a Lutino) exists, though it is extremely rare. It is a magnificent bird, whose red feathers have remained red whereas all the green feathers have become yellow. The head and belly of the young cocks are also yellow to begin with. This Yellow mutation inherits autosomal recessive.
In captivity the red of the adult cock occasionally turns to orange. The reason for this is not known. The young of these birds are coloured normally.

11. Green-winged King Parakeet; the male (left) has a blue back

GREEN-WINGED KING PARAKEET
Alisterus chloropterus

Subspecies

1. *Alisterus chloropterus chloropterus*
Green-winged King Parakeet
2. *Alisterus chloropterus callopterus*
Fly River King Parakeet
3. *Alisterus chloropterus moszkowskii*
Moszkowski King Parakeet

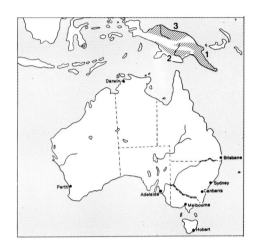

The photograph shows number 3. The hens have virtually no blue on the back. The cocks of number 2 and 3 are very similar; the blue on the backs of cocks of number 1 reaches to the neck, and the wing bar is more yellowish-green. The hens of 1 and 2 look more like those of the Australian King Parakeet; they have green heads and breasts. However, they differ from the Australian in having a little red on the upper mandible.

Origin of name

Alisterus: this genus was named by Gregory M. Mathews, who named it after his son Alister.
Chloropterus: green wing.
Callopterus: beautiful bird.
Moszkowskii: after Dr Max Moszkowski, a German doctor born in 1873 who collected plants and animals from New Guinea and elsewhere as a hobby, and among them these parakeets.
Fly River: river in New Guinea.
Dutch: groenvleugel koningsparkiet.
German: gelbflügel Königssittich.

Parents and young

The difference between the cock and hen of the Moszkowski King Parakeet is clearly shown in the photograph: the hen lacks the blue visible on the back of the cock. Young birds closely resemble the hen, but the light green wing bar is narrower and duller; they also have partially green feathers on the breast. They become sexually mature in their third year. There is still no visible difference in sex between young birds of two years old.

Sizes and weights

Length: 36cm (14in).
Ring size: 7mm.

Habitat and habits

These are birds of the lowland woods and the lower mountain slopes on the islands where they are found. They have a preference for smaller trees and the lower branches of taller trees; they rarely go into the tops.

They are quiet birds by nature and can be easily approached. They are often alone or in groups of two or three.

Diet

Seeds, berries and other wild fruit, nuts, leaves, blossoms are certainly on the menu, and possibly insects and larvae. Their keeper should take it for granted that more fruit and green food must be supplied than for other Australian parakeets. Special attention must be paid to this with newly imported birds.

Nest-site

Little is known about this. In captivity the same box is usually used as for the other King Parakeets: a height of about 180cm (5ft 11in) and a floor area of 25 x 25cm (10 x 10in); the entrance hole should be about 9cm (3.5in) in diameter.

Breeding process

Two or three eggs are laid, which are then incubated for about twenty days. In the recorded cases of breeding, the number of days that the chicks remained in the nest varies rather: forty-two, forty-nine and fifty-six. It is not unusual for the hen to start incubating a second clutch, however, these eggs are not always fertilized.

General remarks

Recently imported birds must be treated very carefully: they come from an area with a warm, wet climate and they are used to fairly soft food. The switch from berries, fruit and ripe seeds to harder food can soon cause intestinal disorders. Therefore, this must be achieved with care. The same applies to the adjustment to our climate with its low temperatures: this must also change very gradually.

Once they are fully adjusted and acclimatized they are strong birds which can survive most winters, and differ very little from the other Australian King Parakeets. This species is only found in aviaries in very limited numbers.

AMBOINA KING PARAKEET - *Alisterus amboinensis*

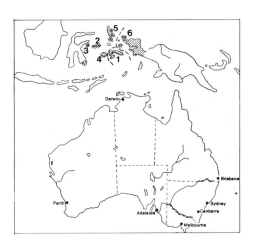

Subspecies
1. *Alisterus amboinensis amboinensis*
   Amboina King Parakeet
2. *Alisterus amboinensis sulaensis*
   Sula King Parakeet
3. *Alisterus amboinensis versicolor*
   Peleng King Parakeet
4. *Alisterus amboinensis buruensis*
   Buru King Parakeet
5. *Alisterus amboinensis hypophonius*
   Blue-winged or Halmahera King Parakeet
6. *Alisterus amboinensis dorsalis*
   Salawati King Parakeet

The photographs show the numbers 1 (Amboina King Parakeet) and 5 (Blue-winged or Halmahera King Parakeet). The most important difference is clearly shown: the first has green wings, the latter has blue. The other subspecies are hardly ever found in captivity; the differences between them are therefore not dealt with.

Origin of names
Alisterus: this genus was named by Gregory M. Mathews, who named it after his son Alister.
Amboinensis: from the island of Ambon.
Sulaensis: from the island of Sula.
Versicolor: of various colours.
Buruensis: from the island of Buru.
Hypophonius: blood-red below.
Dorsalis: relating to the back.
Ambon, Sula, Peleng, Buru, Halmahera, Salawati: Indonesian islands.
Dutch: Ambon koningsparkiet.
German: Ambon Königssittich.

Parents and young
Cocks and hens are very difficult to tell apart. There may be some difference visible on the head and beak. Young birds look similar to adults but they lack the blue on the back; the upper mandible is brownish-black, the lower mandible reddish, and the eye ring is off-white instead of grey. These differences disappear during the first year. They are sexually mature at three years old.

12. Amboina King Parakeet

Sizes and weights
Length: Amboina 41cm (15.5in), Buru 40cm (16in), Halmahera 37cm (14.5in), Salawati 38cm (15in).
Ring size: 7mm.

Habitat and habits
As their names suggest, these birds live only on a number of Indonesian islands. They are therefore not very numerous, and this could be one of the reasons why they are hardly found in collections.
In the wild they live in the same habitat as the Green-winged King Parakeet: lowland woods and the lower mountain slopes. There they quietly search for food amongst the thick foliage and the lower branches either alone or in pairs. They rarely descend to the ground.

Diet
Virtually the same applies as for the Green-winged King Parakeet: seeds, berries and other wild fruit, leaves, blossom, and possibly insects and larvae. The diet in captivity must be based on this: lots of fruit, berries, and green food such as chickweed and spinach, also corncobs.

Nest-site
Amboinas have been bred in nest-boxes 120 to 180cm (4ft to 6ft) tall with floors measuring 25 to 30cm (10 to 12in) square. The entrance hole should have a diameter of about 9cm (3.5in).

Breeding process
Two or three eggs are laid, and incubated by the hen only for about nineteen days. In Denmark a hen laid eggs on 1 and 3 July; both eggs hatched on 21 July, and the chicks fledged on 7 September; so after forty-eight days. In the few other cases the chicks are twice recorded as fledging after fifty-six, and once after sixty-three days. Two clutches are sometimes reared. Breeding does not take place in spring only. When the chicks are fourteen days old the cock begins to feed them, up till then he only feeds the hen. However, it seems that the hen can be fairly aggressive when she has young, and she can even go so far as to kill the cock. It seems, therefore, that the whole process goes better if the cock is removed after some time, so that the hen can concentrate fully on rearing the young birds.

General remarks
The same applies for the Amboina King Parakeet as for the Green-winged King Parakeet: great care must be taken over the birds' adjustment to our climate and food. Once they are acclimatized they can put up with slight frosts.
It can be as much as five years before imported birds start breeding. These parakeets are keen fliers; they hardly ever chew.

13. Halmahera King, a subspecies of the Amboina King Parakeet

Genus *Aprosmictus*

Two species of Crimson-winged Parakeet can be distinguished within this genus, an Australian and an Indonesian form. The plumage is mainly green, with varying amounts of red. There is a much greater difference between the cocks and hens of the Australian species than of the Indonesian. The latter is very rarely found in aviaries. The Indonesian cock has much less red on the wings than the much better known Australian Crimson-wing; the red is replaced by a yellowish-green.

The same applies here as for the King Parakeet: where in the wild the Crimson-wings' range overlaps that of the King Parakeet, the adult cocks and hens differ greatly (numbers 1 and 2); where this is not the case, they are much more alike (numbers 4 and 5; these birds live isolated on the Indonesian islands of Timor and Wetar).

Some experts question the existence of number 3 as a separate subspecies; it is so similar to number 2 that they can also be placed together.

genus	species	subspecies	
Aprosmisctus	*erythropterus*	*erythropterus*	1. Crimson-winged Parakeet
"	"	*coccineopterus*	2. (Lesser) Crimson-winged Parakeet
"	"	*papua*	3. New Guinea Crimson-winged Parakeet
"	*jonquillaceus*	*jonquillaceus*	4. Timor Crimson-winged Parakeet
"	"	*wetterensis*	5. Wetar Crimson-winged Parakeet

14. *Crimson-winged Parakeet; male and female*

CRIMSON-WINGED PARAKEET

Aprosmictus erythropterus

Subspecies

1. *Apromictus erythropterus erythropterus*
   Crimson-winged Parakeet
2. *Aprosmictus erythropterus coccineopterus*
   (Lesser) Crimson-winged Parakeet
3. *Aprosmictus erythropterus papua*
   New Guinea Crimson-winged Parakeet

Number 2 is a little smaller and duller then number 1; number 3 lives in southern New Guinea and is hardly distinguishable from number 2.

In captivity the subspecies are not clearly recognizable, as in the past not enough attention was paid to the forming of breeding pairs.

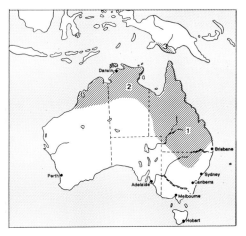

Origin of names

Aprosmictus: not mixing with others, isolated.
Erythropterus: red wing.
Coccineopterus: scarlet wing.
Papua: from Papua.
Dutch: roodvleugelparkiet.
German: Rotflügelsittich.

Parents and young

The cock is distinguishable by its shiny light green head, red wings and black back. Apart from their dark eyes, immature birds look like the hen. It is sometimes possible to determine the sex by the colour of the rump: the cocks' can be a deeper blue. It can only be seen with more certainty at an age of eighteen months or more when the first black feathers on the backs of the cocks start coming through. Some breeders wish to know sooner. They pull out a few back feathers, which are replaced by black ones if it is a cock and green if it is a hen.

They, therefore, take much longer to develop their adult plumage than King Parakeets. The plumage is complete after about two and a half years. In the wild, therefore, they start breeding in their third year. In captivity the hen sometimes starts breeding as early as her second year; the cock must be at least three years old. However, it is not unusual for the birds to miss the third year, and only become active in the fourth.

Sizes and weights
Length: 32cm (12½in).
Weights: cock 120-146g, hen 149g.
Ring size: 6mm.

Habitat and habits
They have a preference for open country with eucalyptus trees and acacia bushes, and for trees along watercourses. Crimson-wings live mainly in trees; they rarely come down to the ground and are seldom far from water. They are common within their range. They live in pairs or in family groups, although, outside the breeding season, groups of as many as fifteen to twenty birds are recorded. They are not easy to approach.

The males are clearly dominant; they are not very courteous to the hens. They rarely show any affection and are more likely to be nasty, although this is not true of all cocks. However, there are those who very aggressively chase after hens. Great care must, therefore, be taken when forming pairs from adult birds, as this does not always go smoothly, particularly if a new hen is being introduced into the aviary of a resident cock.

Pairs must not be housed to close to each other, as the cocks will have more (aggressive) attention for each other than for their own mates, and this can result in breeding failure.

15. Crimson-winged Parakeet; a Pied adult cock and a normal hen

Diet
Crimson-wings eat the seeds of various grasses, bushes (they are particularly fond of acacias), also berries and other wild fruit, blossoms, insects and larvae.

Nest-site
Nests are often found deep in hollow eucalyptus trees which are near water. It is not uncommon for the eggs to be at ground level. In captivity the birds also prefer a tall nest-box, which should have a height of 180 to 200cm (5ft 11in to 6ft 7in).
One of my own pairs refused to use any hanging boxes, and even laid on the floor of the shelter, until I placed in the outside flight a hollow tree trunk which was one metre, seventy (5ft 7in) long, and open at the top but with an entrance hole in the side. This was immediately accepted. The hen always entered through the open top. As there was no bottom in it, she incubated on a layer of rotten wood standing on the floor. In such cases it is important to lay something on the mesh above the block to prevent rain getting in.
Although a number of other reports show that these birds prefer a tall block, breeding success has been achieved with boxes measuring 60 x 25 x 25cm (24 x 10 x 10in).
Clearly though, a certain particularity with regard to nest-sites is not uncommon in the hen, so the keeper should pay special attention to this aspect.

Breeding process
It is my experience that Crimson-wings occasionally start breeding early, which can be a reason to consider placing the boxes as early as the end of February, that is if they have not been hanging all winter.
The three to six eggs are incubated by the hen for about twenty days. She often leaves the nest for a time in the early morning and late in the afternoon to be fed by the cock. The chicks remain in the nest for about thirty-five days, and sometimes a little longer. Occasionally a second clutch is produced, but generally there is only one. I once had three clutches from the same hen in one season, but these were all unfertilized. A breeding season is sometimes skipped.
The cock occasionally chases the hen aggressively in order to get her into the nest box. It goes without saying, therefore, that these birds can only be housed separately in pairs; or so you would think. However, the proof that it is not the only alternative was provided by an aviculturist in the American state of Arizona: he bred six pairs in a single aviary measuring 9 x 4.5 x 2.7 metres without any problems at all!

General remarks
Crimson-wings are sensitive to frost. Compared to other Australian parakeets they are quickly affected by frozen toes, which can result in claws or bits of toes disappearing. In more severe frosts they must, in any case, not spend the night in an open aviary.
They go into moult fairly early, often before most other species.
They do not become as attached to their keepers as the King Parakeets.

Mutations
A Pied Crimson-winged Parakeet exists. The photograph shows a bird which has almost totally yellow wings. The yellow of this bird becomes more extensive with each moult.

Genus *Polytelis*

The three species comprising this genus differ slightly from the other Australian parakeets. They display a certain similarity to the genus *Psittacula* in that; the hen is the dominant mate, the courtship display is similar, they have red beaks, the cocks and hens differ (especially in two of the three), and they have long tails. The middle tail feathers are much longer than the rest, whereas the tail feathers of most Australian parakeets are the same length. Species of *Polytelis* make excellent parents. They are suitable for the inexperienced keeper; breeding is not too difficult, they are not aggressive and can become quite tame, they are hardy birds which are not bothered by our climate, they are not destructive and greenery in the aviary is usually left alone. In the correct circumstances it is possible to breed them in colonies.

genus	species	subspecies	
Polytelis	*swainsonii*	-	1. Barraband Parakeet
"	*anthopeplus*	*anthopeplus*	2. Rock Pebbler Parakeet
"	"	*westralis*	3. (Western) Rock Pebbler Parakeet
"	*alexandrae*	-	4. Princess of Wales Parakeet

BARRABAND PARAKEET - *Polytelis swainsonii*

Subspecies
None.

Origin of name
Polytelis: very delicate, precious.
Swainsonii: William Swainson (1789-1855), an English ornithologist and painter, described this bird for the first time and named it *Polytelis barrabandi* after Jacques Barraband, a French bird painter. However, because the name had already been given to a South American species, the name was later changed to *Polytelis swainsonii*.
Barraband: see under Swainsonii.
Dutch: Barrabandparkiet.
German: Schildsittich.

Parents and young
The cock is easily recognizable by the yellow and red on its throat. Immature birds look like the hen. The green of the young cocks is sometimes a little brighter. This becomes more obvious after the first moult, in the autumn at an age of about three to four months. At about ten months the first red feather or two starts appearing. The full adult plumage has been developed by an age of between eighteen and twenty months. Young cocks start becoming vocal after only a couple of months, hens start later. In the wild the birds are sexually mature by their second year; the same applies for birds in captivity, although one-year-old Barraband hens do occasionally start to breed. However, cocks of this age are not able to fertilize the eggs yet.

Sizes and weights
Length: 40cm (16in).
Weights: cock 133-157g, hen 145-155g.
Ring size: 6mm.

Habitat and habits
Barrabands have a preference for open grassland with large trees, and savannah with bushes. They are generally described as birds which live within only a few miles from a river or watercourse. However, they have occasionally been observed in grain growing areas up to forty miles from water.
Although they only have a limited range, they are nevertheless common within it.

16. Barraband Parakeet; female and male

90

They are found in small flocks throughout the year, and in the breeding season it is not possible to observe any splitting up into pairs. They are most active in the early morning and late afternoon, when they are either on the ground searching for grass seeds or in the trees eating blossom. The rest of the day is spent motionless and quiet in a tree.

They are known among aviculturists as reliable and reasonably tame birds.

Diet

As mentioned above these parakeets spend a lot of time on the ground searching for the seeds of grasses and herbs. They also eat berries, nuts, nectar and blossom.

Nest-site

In Australia Barrabands nest high above the ground. This is impossible in an aviary, but they do not regard this as a problem and breed fairly readily at a height of only one and a half to two metres (5-6ft).

A suitable box measures 60 x 18 x 18cm (24 x 7 x 7in), with an entrance hole of about 8cm (3in) in diameter.

Breeding process

This species often begins courtship early and it can last for several weeks. A clutch numbers four to six eggs, which are incubated for about twenty days before the chicks hatch. For the first few days they are fed only by the hen, but after a week the cock joins in. The chicks fledge after about five weeks. There is usually only one clutch, but every now and then a second follows. In the breeding season the hen is more active than the cock.

General remarks

The flight must not be too short, as Barrabands tend to become overweight. Therefore, they must be able to fly freely.

They are social birds by nature, and better breeding results can often be achieved by keeping a number of pairs. These need not necessarily be placed in one aviary, as the neighbouring birds' sound and behaviour are enough to encourage each other.

The hen is the dominant mate.

This species is susceptible to paralysis of the legs and eye infections. Paralysis can sometimes suddenly occur as the result of shock or stress. It is difficult to cure. In some cases it disappears of its own accord. Eye infections should be treated with a antibiotic cream. See also chapter VIII.

17. Rock Pebbler Parakeet; female and male

ROCK PEBBLER PARAKEET - *Polytelis anthopeplus*

Subspecies
1. *Polytelis anthopeplus anthopeplus*
               Rock Pebbler Parakeet
2. *Polytelis anthopeplus westralis*
               (Western) Rock Pebbler Parakeet

Besides the nominate form (number 1) there is only one - disputable - subspecies. As can be seen from the map, Rock Pebbler Parakeets are found in two widely separated areas in Australia: number 1 in the southeast and number 2 in the southwest. The male birds in the southwest are on the whole less yellow than those in the southeast. However, birds are seen in the southwest which come up to their far neighbours' colouring. There is doubt, therefore, if one can really speak of a subspecies. The hens from the two areas are alike.

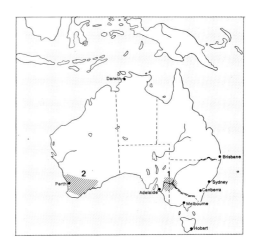

Also in captivity we find birds with varying amounts of yellow. However, these are not members of the two pure subspecies, as these have been crossbred on a large scale.

Origin of name
Polytelis: very delicate, precious.
Anthopeplus: flowered female gown.
Westralis: western.
Dutch: bergparkiet.
German: Bergsittich.

Parents and young
The cock is predominantly yellow and the hen olive green. Immature cocks and hens are difficult to tell apart, although sometimes with birds from the same clutch the colour of the cocks is already a little brighter. At about eight months they begin to turn more yellow. This process continues until they have developed their adult plumage at between fourteen and eighteen months.

Just like other birds of this genus, in the wild Rock Pebbler Parakeets are sexually mature by the end of their second year. In captivity it is not unusual for a one-year-old hen to lay eggs. However, these are almost never fertilized if the cock is of the same age. Chicks can only be reared when the cock is two or more years old.

Sizes and weights
Length: 40cm (16in).
Weights: cock 170g, hen 175g.
Ring size: 6mm.

Habitat and habits

The Rock Pebbler Parakeet inhabits open woodland, trees lining roads and watercourses, fields of cereals, orchards, and areas with bush-like eucalyptuses to a height of three metres (ten feet). In the wild they are usually found in pairs or small groups, although flocks of three to four hundred birds are occasionally seen. At night they roost in trees along the banks of watercourses. During the day they display the behaviour which is common to many species of parakeet in the wild: they search for food in the morning, spend the rest of the day resting in the cover of trees or dense scrub near the feeding places, eat again as evening approaches and then leave for their roost, where they first drink again before sleeping.

They are strong fliers, although they are less active than, for example, the Barrabands.

Diet

Rock Pebbler Parakeets like to eat eucalyptus and acacia seeds, wild fruit, but will also take the seeds of a variety of grasses and herbs, berries, nuts, leaf buds, blossom, and greenery. They spend a lot of time on the ground when foraging.

18. Rock Pebbler Parakeet; an entirely Yellow-backed cock

94

Nest-site

They have a clear preference for holes in eucalyptuses along watercourses. These can be dead or living trees. It is not unusual for a number of pairs to nest in the same area. Sometimes a number of nests are even found in one tree. The entrance to the nest can be up to twelve metres (thirty-nine feet) above the ground, and the eggs may be five metres (twenty feet) lower. The parents usually return to the same nest every year.

In captivity a hanging nest box 60cm (24in) long and 20cm (8in) square is sufficient. The diameter of the entrance hole should be about 8½cm (3½in).

Breeding process

It is characteristic of the Rock Pebbler Parakeet that early in the spring the hen starts begging the cock for food. She often sits on the perch in the mating position. If the cock is not yet sexually mature it will pay no attention to the hen. However, she often lays eggs nevertheless, which is why unfertilized eggs are sometimes found. If these are removed in time, there is a fairly good chance of a second clutch of fertilized eggs.

The three to six eggs are incubated by the hen for about twenty days. But there are exceptions to this as proved by a German breeder who had a hen with ten fertilized eggs who reared all ten chicks!

During the incubation period the hen is fed by the cock, usually outside the box. Once the chicks have hatched she looks after them alone for about two weeks; after that the cock also enters the box to feed the young. This goes on until the chicks are about thirty-five days old and leave the box; then their parents help in their feeding for at least another three weeks. There is no objection to letting them remain together at first; however, if the parents start showing signs of breeding a second time, it is not a bad idea to remove the young birds as they will keep begging for food for a long time to come and this could unnecessarily distract the parents' attention from a second round.

Breeding in colonies in the aviary is a possibility. The aviary must be sufficiently large and there must be more nest-boxes than pairs of birds. It is preferable to have the same number of cocks and hens. I have personally bred Rock Pebbler, Princess of Wales and Indian Ringnecks successfully together in an aviary with an outside flight measuring three by seven metres (ten by twenty-three feet) without any problems. However, a number of pairs in separate flights can also have a favourable effect on each other.

General remarks

The build of Rock Pebbler Parakeets varies somewhat. Some birds appear rather plump, whereas others look exceptionally graceful. With the exception of the mornings and evenings they are not very active.

These birds do not bathe in standing water, and are therefore dependent on rain for washing. They require a flight which is at least four metres (13ft) long.

The hen is usually the boss; however, she is not aggressive, so this never gives rise to problems.

The paralysis and eye infections mentioned for the Barraband can also affect this species. See chapter VIII.

Mutations

One of the photographs shows a Rock Pebbler with a completely yellow back. At the time of writing it is not entirely clear which mutation or colour variation is involved, as too few offspring have so far been bred to be able to draw any conclusions from the results.

19. Princess of Wales Parakeet; this bird is recognizable as a cock by the elongations on the points of the wings, the so-called spatula

PRINCESS OF WALES PARAKEET - *Polytelis alexandrae*

Subspecies
None.

Origin of name
Polytelis: very delicate, precious.
Alexandrae: in 1863 John Gould named this bird after Princess Alexandra, the Queen of Denmark's daughter and married to the Prince of Wales. They later became King (Edward VII) and Queen of England.
Dutch: Prinses van Walesparkiet.
German: Princess of Walessittich.

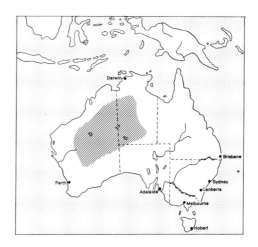

Parents and young
The sexes of older birds are fairly easily determined. The cock's clearest distinguishing feature is the slightly longer third primary feather, the so-called spatula. The hen does not have this.
If this spatula is not visible, make quite sure of the bird's sex by looking for the following differences, as this elongation sometimes falls off. The rump of the cock is violetish-blue, and that of the hen greyish-blue. Furthermore, the beak of the cock is redder, the blue on the head is deeper, and the tail feathers are longer. Young cocks can start displaying and 'singing' after only a few months. One of the aspects of the display is the dilating and contracting of the pupil, which causes the red of the iris to become alternately large and small. The difference between young birds is otherwise fairly difficult to see; they all look like the hen. They develop their full adult plumage after fifteen to eighteen months. They normally show the first signs of breeding activity when they are two years old; occasionally they succeed when they are only one year old.

Sizes and weights
Length: 45cm (17½in).
Weights: cock 92g.
Ring size: 6mm.

Habitat and habits
Central Australia contains the second largest desert region in the world; however, a certain amount of vegetation does grow there. There are extensive plains on which Spinifex grass grows, and also areas with eucalyptus trees and acacia bushes. The larger trees line the scarce watercourses. This vast deserted region forms the habitat of the Princess.
These parakeets are very nomadic, and are rarely to be found in one place for very long, mainly because they have to follow their food and water supply, which is only available

20. Blue Princess of Wales Parakeet

when rain falls. However, this does not happen very often and is difficult to forecast, and this makes it a hopeless task to try and track down these birds in this vast desert. It is no wonder then, that the Princess is regarded as a rare and threatened species. As so little is known about them, the situation might not be too bad, although according to the Atlas of Australian Birds this parakeet was last seen in the wild in 1981.

Princesses usually move round in pairs or in small groups, and occasionally in larger flocks. They are most active in the morning and evening, when they forage about on the ground in search of seeds. The remainder of the day they can sit for long periods with their heads tucked into their feathers. This sometimes leads to anxiety among some aviculturists because the birds give the impression of being ill. Usually there is nothing wrong.

It is often the hen that wears the 'trousers', so to speak; the cock spends most of the year trying to get her affection.

Diet

Large amounts of seeds of grasses and herbs are eaten which grow on or just above the ground; also berries and other wild fruit, blossoms, and insects and larvae.

Nest-site

In the wild Princesses search out breeding sites in areas where it has just rained and where there will be sufficient food and water for a number of weeks. They may not reappear at such places for dozens of years. They take to the trees when nesting, and there are often a number of nests in the same area. There is a report of ten nests being found in one tree!

In the aviary boxes measuring 60 x 20 x 20cm (24 x 8 x 8ins) are used. It is not uncommon for eggs to get broken and on the assumption that the hen breaks the eggs by letting herself fall onto the nest, many birdkeepers prefer to hang the box sloping at an angle, which means that the hen has to walk down to the nest. However, judging by the experiences of several other birdkeepers, it seems more probable that it is due to the cock entering the box and 'playing football' with them. If you have problems with this, there are several possibilities for its prevention: the first is to remove the cock temporarily from the aviary when the hen starts to lay; secondly, the entrance hole can be made smaller with, for example, a piece of tree bark, the hen will then chew an opening just big enough to get in, and as the cock is a little bigger it will not be able to enter so easily; finally, the eggs can be replaced by artificial ones immediately after laying, and then put back once the hen starts to incubate. The diameter of the entrance hole should be 7cm (3ins).

Breeding process

Three to seven eggs are laid and incubated by the hen for about twenty days. Some cocks feed the hens during this period, others show little or no interest. The young leave the box after about five weeks. In the wild the parents and young leave the breeding area virtually immediately. In captivity the family can remain intact.

Two clutches a year are no longer regarded as exceptions. If this occurs, care must be taken that the young of the first clutch do not distract the parents too much. If this happens it is better to remove them.

Just as by previous species it is possible to breed in colonies. If there are a number of

21. Princess of Wales Parakeet; Lutino cock and hen

pairs they stimulate each other by their calls; therefore, they do not necessarily need to be housed in the same aviary.

General remarks

The Princess has all the characteristics of a perfect aviary bird: friendly, tame, easy to sex, good to breed, and a feast for the eye. Also, our climate does not present any problems, despite the fact that this parakeet originates from one of the hottest regions in Australia.

It is sometimes regarded as a disadvantage that Princesses are not very active, and spend the greater part of the day on the perch with their heads buried in their feathers. However, not all birds show this behaviour. I myself have had Princesses which, in this respect, behaved just like the majority of other Australians.

It could well be that there are more Princesses in captivity than there are in the wild in Australia.

Putting smaller, non-aggressive species in with Princesses does not normally cause any problems.

Just as with the Barraband and the Rock Pebbler Parakeet this bird is rather susceptible to eye infections. See chapter VIII.

Mutations

So far we have the Blue, Lutino, and Albino Princess. The Blue is the most common; the mode of inheritance is autosomal recessive. The mode of inheritance of the Lutino is, as opposed to most other lutinos, also autosomal recessive, and the Albino also has this mode of inheritance. The Albino can be bred from a combination of lutino and blue; see chapter VII. ··

22. Albino Princess of Wales Parakeet; can be bred indirectly from Blue and Lutino

Genus *Purpureicephalus*

This genus comprises one species only, which is strikingly different to other Australian parakeets in a number of ways.

As a result of its eating habits, the beak is exceptionally long.

The plumage is a distinctive lively assortment of superb colours, and the courtship display has a unique form.

There has been much discussion about the position of the Red-capped Parrot in the system, and eventually the general conclusion was reached that this species could not be included into any other genus and should be regarded as separate.

genus	species	subspecies	
Purpureicephalus	*spurius*	-	Red-capped Parrot

23. *Red-capped Parrot; the cock on the left has a deeper red on its head and purplish-blue on its breast. Some hens are less beautiful than this one and have more green on the head.*

RED-CAPPED PARROT - *Purpureicephalus spurius*

Subspecies
None.

Origin of name
Purpureicephalus: purple head.
Spurius: not genuine.
Dutch: roodkapparkiet.
German: Rotkappensittich.

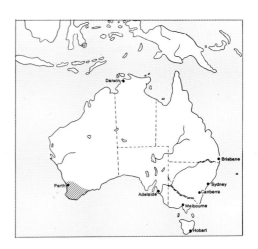

Parents and young
The colouring of adult Red-capped Parrot hens varies greatly. Some are almost as colourful as the cock, and others are much duller and have an almost entirely green head; these look very similar to immature birds. Be careful, therefore, when purchasing this species: there are also hens with a beautiful red cap! Pay attention to a number of other points as well. The head is often smaller and rounder, whereas when viewed from the side the cock's is much longer; in most cases the beak of the cock is also a little larger. Although a white stripe on the underside of the wing cannot be considered an infallible indication of sex, an adult bird bearing it is most likely to be a hen. By the same tqken, a bird without the stripe is not necessarily a cock.
Red-capped Parrots develop their adult plumage in twelve to sixteen months. From this can be deduced that they do not usually breed in their first year, but must be two years old.
In order to breed handsome birds it is advisable to choose the most colourful hens for mothers. The risk of getting two cocks in the aviary is, however, greater.

Sizes and weights
Length: 37cm (15in).
Weights: cock 105-156g, hen 98-135g.
Ring size: 6mm.

Habitat and habits
The distribution range in the southwest of Australia is fairly small; the birds inhabit various sorts of landscape within this range, ranging from dense eucalyptus forests to more open areas with trees growing round cultivated land or along roads and watercourses; they are even found in parks and orchards. The presence of two types of eucalyptuses is of particular importance, as these parakeets have a marked preference for their seeds.
They are common in the wild. Adult birds usually live in pairs, whereas immature birds group together in flocks of twenty or more.

24. *Red-capped Parrot; this young bird is not yet displaying the splendid colours of its parents*

106

Red-capped Parrots are very active and fly a great deal. As this keeps them in top condition, the aviary should be at least five metres (16ft) long. It is best to house them somewhere peaceful, as they are shy birds by nature; despite the many years of breeding in captivity, apart from the occasional exception, they show little sign of losing this shyness.

They are rather aggressive and intolerant. Therefore, give each pair plenty of room to themselves and do not put any other birds in with them.

Diet

In the wild Red-capped Parrots mainly feed on the fruits of two types of eucalyptus trees. They remove the seeds from these urn- shaped fruits with their specially shaped beaks. The seeds of various other trees and bushes help to keep the wolf from the door and they also eat nectar. In the aviary they need quite a lot of fruit, green food, and seeding grass, and there are keepers that give them honey. They will sometimes catch insects for dessert.

Nest-site

In the aviary a 60 to 70cm (24 to 48in) high nest-box with a floor measuring 20 x 20cm (8 x 8in) is sufficient. However, there are aviculturists that use taller boxes; sometimes even as tall as 120cm (4ft). The entrance hole should have a diameter of 7.5cm (3in). In the wild the nest is usually high up in a tree.

Breeding process

The cock puts a lot of work into his courtship display; he shows all his colours to their best advantage and raises his red crown feathers. If he gets on well enough with his mate, she will lay four to seven eggs, which will be incubated for about twenty days. On account of the nervous nature of these birds, any nest inspections should be gone about very carefully. The hen is easily disturbed and will then abandon the nest, so make sure that the nest site is peaceful..

Although the cock does help with feeding the chicks in the box, he only starts this when they are a few weeks old. If all goes well the fledglings emerge after about five weeks. Afterwards they are, of course, fed for some time by the parents. Although in the wild the family can remain together for up to a year, in captivity it is better to remove the young from the parents after some time. The limited space at their disposal presents too many risks if the father should become aggressive.

It can be as late as May before the first eggs are laid, and there is usually only one clutch.

General remarks

Red-capped Parrots are keen bathers, so a large dish of water should always be present.

Another characteristic is their love of chewing; they can cause quite a lot of damage in the aviary with their strong beaks. Therefore, give them plenty of branches and if they start attacking the frame of the aviary, attach planks to it which they can chew to their hearts' desire without destroying their home.

Low temperatures in winter do not present any problems; these birds are exceptionally hardy. Take their shyness into account and do not think that they will lose it. This is the case with various other parakeets, but less likely with Redcaps. Another, less pleasant, characteristic is that sometimes without warning a bird is suddenly found dead in the aviary, with no apparent cause. Such birds appear well-nourished and the day before were still fully active. An adequate explanation for this has not yet been given.

Genus *Barnardius*

Although many aviculturists think that this genus consists of four species, there are in fact only two. The Cloncurry is a subspecies of the Barnard, and the Twenty -eight is a subspecies of the Port Lincoln. The first two have green heads and are found in the eastern part of Australia, the last two have black heads and inhabit the western part.

There are two with a red band on the forehead (Barnard and Twenty-eight) and two with virtually none (Cloncurry and Port Lincoln).

The differences between the sexes are slight and this can sometimes raise problems for the aviculturist.

The four birds mentioned have a special place as aviary bird and these are, therefore, dealt with separately. There are two more subspecies which are less clearly distinguishable, and they are included by the relevant species.

genus	species	subspecies	
Barnardius	*barnardius*	*barnardi*	1. Barnard's Parakeet
"	"	*whitei*	2. Barnard's Parakeet
"	"	*macgillivrayi*	3. Cloncurry Parakeet
"	*zonarius*	*zonarius*	4. Port Lincoln Parakeet
"	"	*semitorquatus*	5. Twenty-eight Parakeet
"	"	*occidentalis*	6.(Western) Port Lincoln Parakeet

BARNARD'S PARAKEET

Barnardius barnardius barnardi

Subspecies

1. *Barnardius barnardius barnardi*
    Barnard's Parakeet
2. *Barnardius barnardius whitei*
    Barnard's Parakeet
3. *Barnardius barnardius macgillivrayi*
    Cloncurry Parakeet

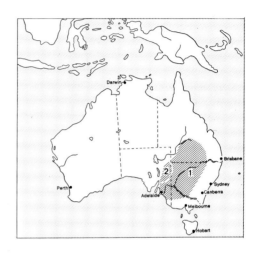

The Cloncurry Parakeet is dealt with separately next, so no mention is made of it here. Of the remaining two, number 2 is a little smaller; the green is duller and the mantle and back are greyish-green to darkgreen, while the head is brownish. Number 1 has got an almost black back and a greener head. In captivity these subspecies are difficult to distinguish from each other, as the existence of the differences between the subspecies is hardly ever taken into account when forming pairs.

Origin of name

Barnardius: Edward Barnard (1786-1861) was a high-ranking civil servant in the British Crown colonies who was deeply interested in flora and fauna.
Whitei: Samual Albert White (1870-1954) was born in Adelaide. He made many expeditions into the Australian interior in search of birds.
Dutch: Barnardparkiet.
German: Barnardsittich.

Parents and young

The whole of the plumage of the hen is duller than that of the cock. Her mantle and back are greyish-green, whereas the cock's are a deep bluish-black. However you must take care, for there is a lot of variation in the colouring of adult birds, particularly on the back and in the orange-yellow band on the belly. Many birdkeepers prefer the cocks to have a broad yellow band and as black a back as possible. The head of the hen tends towards brown instead of green. The head and beak of the cock are visibly larger. Many adult hens have a white stripe under the wings, but cocks never do.
Immature birds look very similar to the hen; the top of their heads and napes are brownish. The full adult plumage develops after twelve to eighteen months, so the cocks have lost their wing stripes by then. A one-year-old hen does occasionally breed, but normally the birds must be two years old.

25. *Barnard's Parakeet; this cock is more brightly coloured, has more green on his head and a larger bill than the hen. She often has a brownish-grey tint on her crown*

Sizes and weights
Length: 35cm (14in).
Weights: cock 111-143g, hen 105-138g.
Ring size: 6mm.

Habitat and habits
The Australian name for the Barnard's Parakeet is Mallee Ring-necked Parrot. This refers to the sort of countryside the bird prefers. 'Mallee' is the name given to various types of eucalyptus which are found in dry regions and which have a bushlike appearance. They cannot be said to have one trunk, but rather many trunks sprouting out of the soil.
However, Barnard's Parakeets can also be found in open woodland and in trees around cultivated land and along watercourses.
They are reasonably common and live mostly in pairs, or in small groups of parents and young birds. They can be seen on the ground searching for food or on the ends of the branches of eucalyptus trees. They spend the hottest part of the day resting. Their aggressive nature prevents them from being housed with others in one aviary.

Diet
Their diet consists of the seeds of grasses and herb-like plants, leaves, blossom, berries and other wild fruit, insects and larvae.

Nest-site
Just as most other parakeets the nests can be found in holes in trees, not too far from water. It is the hen which makes the final choice. A suitable box measures 60 x 20 x 20cm (24 x 8 x 8in), and the diameter of the entrance hole should be 6cm (2½in).

Breeding process
A clutch numbers four to six eggs, although I once had a two-year-old hen which laid eight. The incubating time is about nineteen days, and after the chicks have hatched they remain in the box for about five weeks.
The hen leaves the nest in the early morning and late afternoon to eat and be fed by the cock. He often sits in wait in the vicinity of the box.
In the wild the young remain with their parents for some months after they have fledged.

General remarks
Barnard's Parakeets can be fairly aggressive. The hen has even been known to kill her mate on occasion. Though it must be said that they can both look after themselves.
As the colouring of this species is rather variable, it is advisable to buy birds which match each other. Some Barnard's Parakeets are pure green, whereas others are more of a bluish-green, in which the blue can even be dominant; and there is a whole range of shades in between, which presents every aviculturist with the opportunity to express his own taste. Our climate presents no problems; they can be kept without any heating, though of course with the required shelter in winter.

Mutations
A pure Blue mutation exists, from which the yellow has disappeared; the effect is most visible in the white bands on the nape and belly. The mode of inheritance is autosomal recessive.

26. Blue Barnard Parakeet

CLONCURRY PARAKEET
Barnardius barnardius macgillivrayi

Subspecies
As already mentioned, the Cloncurry Parakeet is a subspecies of the Barnard's Parakeet. As can be seen from the photographs, the colouring of the Cloncurry is much softer and the red band on the forehead is missing.

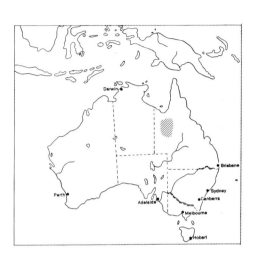

Origin of name
Barnardius: Edward Barnard (1786-1861) was a high-ranking civil servant in the British Crown colonies who was deeply interested in flora and fauna.
Macgillivrayi: Alexander Sykes Macgillivray (1853-1907) was an Australian farmer who went on many expeditions into the interior, where he discovered this bird.
Cloncurry: town in Australia, in the region in which this parakeet is found.
Dutch: Cloncurryparkiet.
German: Cloncurrysittich

Parents and young
The cock and hen look very alike. The colours of the hen are a little less deep and the head and beak of the cock are heavier.
The young look a lot like the parents, but are paler; they have an orange-yellow band on the forehead, the clarity of which varies and which disappears after a few months. They gain their adult plumage at fourteen to eighteen months. Although one-year-old birds do occasionally breed, two years is generally regarded as normal.

Sizes and weights
Length: 33cm (13in).
Weights: cock 120-128g, hen 99-106g.
Ring size: 6mm.

Habitat and habits
The habitat varies from fairly dry undulating regions to large areas of open grassland, open woodlands, dense scrub, and larger watercourses. They have a clear preference for tall eucalyptus trees along such watercourses and in this respect their habits differ from the Barnard's Parakeet. Their behaviour is otherwise very similar, although they are a little less active and make less noise. They fly round in pairs or in family groups.

27. *Cloncurry Parakeet; the bill of the cock (left) is visibly larger*

Diet
Their food consists mainly of the seeds of grasses and herb-like plants; they also eat leaves, wild fruit, berries, insects and larvae.

Nest-site
This is a little different to the Barnard's Parakeet's. These birds are possibly a little less particular in their choice of a nest- box. Generally speaking they accept any box that is between 40 and 100cm (1ft 4in and 3ft 3in) tall and has a floor measuring 20cm (8in) square. The diameter of the entrance hole should be 6cm (2.5in).

Breeding process
A clutch numbers four to six eggs, which are incubated for about twenty days just like the Barnard's Parakeet. After the eggs hatch the cock initially feeds the hen, and the hen feeds the chicks. The cock enters the box to do this, also when the hen is still incubating. Good pairs sometimes have two clutches.

General remarks
Not all pairs get on with each other very well. If this is the case, it is advisable to split the pair up and to place them with other mates in the hope that they are more compatible.
They bear the cold well.
The Cloncurry shows a great similarity to the Barnard's Parakeet in many respects.

28. Port Lincoln Parakeet; the cock (left) has a flatter head and a heavier bill

PORT LINCOLN PARAKEET

Barnardius zonarius zonarius

Subspecies

1. *Barnardius zonarius zonarius*
          Port Lincoln Parakeet
2. *Barnardius zonarius semitorquatus*
          Twenty-eight Parakeet
3. *Barnardius zonarius occidentalis*
          (Western) Port Lincoln Parakeet

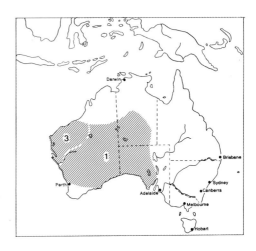

The Twenty-eight Parakeet is dealt with seperately next, so I will restrict myself here to numbers 1 and 3. These look very much alike, but the latter is slightly paler; the head is a pale greyish-black and the cheeks are pale blue. Moreover, it is a little smaller.

The same applies here as for some other subspecies in that they have not been systematically separately bred, which means that it is often difficult to regard birds in captivity as pure. The most recognizably pure is number 1, as it is the most colourful and aviculturists often try to pair the most beautiful birds with each other.

Origin of name

Barnardius: Edward Barnard (1786-1861) was a high-ranking civil servant in the British Crown colonies who was deeply interested in flora and fauna.

Zonarius: with bands or rings.

Occidentalis: western.

Port Lincoln: harbour in southern Australia.

Dutch: Port Lincolnparkiet.

German: Bauer's Ringsittich.

Parents and young

Cocks and hens are very similar in appearance; the head of the hen is sometimes more brownish-black than black, the head and beak may be smaller, and the hen often has a slighter build.

Whether there is a wing bar or not is not a totally reliable indication of sex. Adult birds which have a stripe on the underwing are hens, however there are hens without stripes. A good Port Lincoln has not got any red above the beak.

Young birds are a little duller, but on the whole they resemble their parents. The only way to sex them is to study their heads and beaks. They develop their adult plumage by the time they are eighteen months old. They are sexually mature after two years, which means that they do not usually breed the first year.

Sizes and weights
Length: 37cm (14½in).
Weights: cock 142-170g, hen 121-136g.
Ring size: 6mm.

Habitat and habits
The Port Lincoln is a bird which adapts fairly easily and, therefore, is found in a variety of landscapes: dense woods by the coast, dryish eucalyptus woods, regions with acacia, casuarina and eucalyptus bushes, and also near fields of cereals. They are very often found near water, as they are not able to go without it for long. This is also why in most cases they nest in tall trees along watercourses. Within the range mentioned they are fairly common to very common, and are the most widespread and best-known parakeets in western Australia. They are found in pairs or in small flocks, often foraging on the ground or in the branches of trees and bushes.

Diet
Seeds, berries and other fruits, nuts, nectar, blossom, leaves, insects and larvae are all included on the menu.

Nest-site
The Port Lincoln has a lot in common with the Barnard's Parakeet regarding its nesting habits. The nest is often made in the taller eucalyptuses along watercourses; it is chosen by the hen. In the wild the entrance hole can be as much as fifteen metres (50ft) above ground, the diameter of the cavity is often not more than 20cm (8in).
In the aviary the box should have a height of between 60 and 75cm (2 and 3ft); a floor size of 20 x 20cm (8 x 8in) is sufficient. An entrance hole measuring a good 7cm (3in) is enough to admit the birds.

Breeding process
The first eggs can be laid as early as March. It is, therefore, a good idea to see to it that the birds have a nest-box available in good time. I have heard aviculturists state that the presence of a box in the late autumn and winter sometimes has a stimulating effect. I myself have seen the hen busy with the box as early as October. The cock can start feeding the hen as early as January.
The size of the clutch is usually four to seven, and eggs are incubated for about twenty days. At first the chicks are only fed by the hen, and after ten days to a fortnight by the cock. After leaving the nest five weeks later, the young birds in the wild remain with their parents for several months.

General remarks
Port Lincolns often come down to the floor of their aviary. They are hardy birds and are long-lived. They are rather prone to chewing.
As they are good fliers, an aviary five metres (16ft 6in) long is certainly no luxury. In the wild crossbreeding occurs with other species and sub-species of the genus *Barnardius*, of course only in the places where their ranges overlap.
The call of the Port Lincoln consists of two syllables, and that of the Twenty-eight of three.

TWENTY-EIGHT PARAKEET
Barnardius zonarius semitorquatus

Subspecies

The Twenty-eight is a subspecies of the Port Lincoln. Sometimes two forms of the Twenty-eight are mentioned: a yellow and a green one. This refers to the colour of the belly. The green one is the only true form.

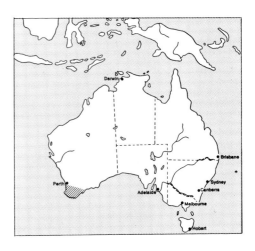

The green on the belly of this bird is slightly lighter than that on the breast, and the division is fairly clear. The so-called yellow Twenty-eight has a yellow belly, and in that respect closely resembles the Port Lincoln. However, this bird is nothing other than a cross between a Twenty-eight and a Port Lincoln (which, by the way, also occurs in the wild). Therefore, always buy only pure-bred birds; either Port Lincolns (yellow belly and no red above the beak) or green Twenty-eights (green belly and a red band on the forehead). The Twenty-eight is slightly more heavily-built and larger than the Port Lincoln.

Origin of name

Barnardius: Edward Barnard (1786-1861) was a high-ranking civil servant in the British Crown colonies who was deeply interested in flora and fauna.
Zonarius: with bands or rings.
Semitorquatus: half collared.
Twenty-eight: refers to the birds' call (just like the cuckoo), which consists of three syllables. This is also true of the Barnardius zonarius occidentalis, but the Port Lincoln has a call of two syllables.
Dutch: twenty-eightparkiet.
German: Kragensittich.

Parents and young

For the most part the hen looks similar to the cock. However, her colours are a little duller and the head is sometimes brown rather than black; moreover, the red band on the forehead is narrower. Hens' heads are smaller and rounder, and their beaks are smaller. The heads of the cocks are larger and more angular and the upper mandible is heavier. Adult birds which have a row of white spots or a stripe on the underside of their wings are almost certainly hens. However, there are probably hens without these markings.
Immature birds resemble the hen very closely; their colouring is generally slightly duller, and the red band on the forehead is often smaller and narrower.
In the wild Twenty-eights are sexually mature after two years. In captivity one-year-old birds sometimes rear young, but this is more the exception than the rule.

29. Twenty-eight Parakeet; the cock (left) is more heavily-built, particularly the head and beak

Sizes and weights
Length: 40cm (16in).
Weights: cock 142-191g, hen 134-199g.
Ring size: 6mm.

Habitat and habits
In this respect Twenty-eights show a great resemblance to Port Lincolns. However, they do spend more time in trees. Of all the *Barnardius* species they are the ones that live in the wettest region, where trees grow to a height of eighty-five metres (280ft). As a result they generally fly higher than their relations. For further information please refer to the Port Lincoln.

Diet
This too is similar to that of the Port Lincoln. They have a preference for the seeds and fruits of many types of eucalyptus trees.

Nest-site
In many cases Port Lincolns nest at a very great height. This site is, of course, impossible to reconstruct in an aviary. Luckily it is not necessary, as they will settle for a nest box hanging much nearer the ground. This should be about 70cm (2ft 4in) tall and a good 20cm (8in) square. The entrance hole must be slightly larger than for Port Lincolns: about 8cm (3.5in).

Breeding process
Four to seven eggs are laid which then have to be incubated for about twenty-one days before the young hatch. During this period the hen is fed by the cock, usually in the close vicinity of the nest.
When the chicks are a few days old the cock helps in feeding them. The clutch emerges into the outside world after about five weeks.

General remarks
Of all the (sub)species of *Barnardius* this is more difficult to breed. It is an aggressive bird, which should not be housed with or next to other species of *Barnardius* or *Platycercus*. They are rather prone to chewing, and are even capable of destroying wire mesh. This should, therefore, be checked regularly.
Five metres (16ft 6in) should be regarded as the minimum length of the flight for these quite large birds. Just as for others of the *Barnardius* genus, our climate does not present any problems, as long as there is at least a weatherproof shelter available.

Mutations
A Blue Twenty-eight has been bred. It inherits autosomal recessive. This bird is still very rare.

Genus *Platycercus*

This genus forms a very separate group. The birds within it are known among aviculturists as Rosellas. Their main distinguishing feature is the colouring on their backs; every back feather has a black centre and a coloured edge which matches the general colour of the rest of the plumage, and produces a scale-like pattern. They also have conspicuous patches on their cheeks. They have a habit of shaking their spread tails, especially during the courtship display.

Rosellas are long-lived birds and are generally fairly good breeders. They are, however, aggressive and it is better not to house them next to species of the *Barnardius* or *Psephotus* genuses.

Not all the experts are in agreement about the origin of the name Rosella. The general opinion is that it is derived from Rose Hill, the region in which the bird is supposed to have first been seen, and which is now part of Sydney. The theory is that the Rosella was once called a 'Rose-hiller'.

The colours and sizes of birds of the same species vary quite considerably. The species can be divided into as many as twenty-seven geographical varieties. However, generally speaking eight species are recognized, although dicussions occasionally arise about whether the Pennant's Parakeet, Yellow Rosella and the Adelaide Rosella should be accepted as separate species or not. These three have so much in common that they could possibly be considered as being one species. However, the most widely accepted classification into three species is used here.

The eight species can be divided into three groups:

a. Pennant's - Adelaide - Yellow - Yellow-bellied. These are the four largest species. The colouring of the parents and young differs greatly. Young birds are mainly green. All four have a blue cheek patch; the cocks have no wing bar, and the hens sometimes a faint one. They are typically woodland birds which inhabit eastern and southeastern Australia, including Tasmania;

b. Rosella - Mealy - Brown's. The young of these look much more like their parents; they are a little duller and, therefore, do not actually have a separate immature plumage. The cocks have no wing bar, the hens often do; the cheek patch of these species is white. They can be found in northern and eastern Australia, including Tasmania;

c. Stanley. This is only found in southwestern Australia isolated from all the other species. It is the only species in which the cock and hen differ greatly and is also the only one with yellow cheek patches. The cocks have no wing bar, but the hen does; young birds have much more green than their parents.

genus	species	subspecies	
Platycercus	*caledonicus*	-	1. Yellow-bellied Rosella
"	*elegans*	*elegans*	2. Pennant's Parakeet
"	"	*nigrescens*	3. (Northern) Pennant's Parakeet
"	"	*melanoptera*	4. (Kangaroo Island) Pennant's Parakeet
"	*flaveolus*	-	5. Yellow Rosella
"	*adelaidae*	*adelaidae*	6. Adelaide Rosella
"	"	*subadelaidae*	7. Adelaide Rosella
"	*eximius*	*eximius*	8. Eastern Rosella
"	"	*cecilae*	9. Golden-mantled Rosella
"	"	*diemenensis*	10. Tasmanian Rosella
"	*adscitus*	*adscitus*	11. Blue-cheeked Rosella
"	"	*palliceps*	12. Mealy Rosella
"	*venustus*	-	13. Brown's Parakeet
"	*icterotis*	*icterotis*	14. Stanley Parakeet
"	"	*xanthogenys*	15. (Yellow-cheeked) Stanley Parakeet

30. *Yellow-bellied Rosella; cock with a tidy, smooth plumage*

YELLOW-BELLIED ROSELLA - *Platycercus caledonicus*

Subspecies
None. This species, which only inhabits the island of Tasmania, displays some variation in colour. The birds of the rainforest on the west coast are greenish, whereas those from the drier east coast are much yellower. The green birds always seem to have a more ruffled appearance.

Origin of name
Platycercus: flat or broad tail.
Caledonicus: from (New) Caledonia. This is a misnomer, as the Yellow-bellied Rosella is not found there.
Dutch: geelbuikrosella.
German: Gelbbauchsittich.

Parents and young
Cocks and hens have the same colouring. Hens are often slightly smaller and their heads and beaks are usually less heavily built than the cocks'. Cocks do not have wing bars, and neither do hens. Both sometimes have and orange-red tinge to their throats and upper breasts, which is a feature that can also be found in Yellow Rosellas.
The parents' yellow is still olive green on young birds and their backs are duller, which makes the scale-like pattern fainter than in adults. The adult plumage appears after the first total moult at about fifteen months. This is also when they start to reach sexual aturity, so they are able to breed at the end of their second year.

Sizes and weights
Length: 37cm (14.5in).
Weights: cock 105-165g, hen 90-130g.
Ring size: 6mm.

Habitat and habits
Yellow-bellied Rosellas can be found throughout the whole of Tasmania. Their habitat ranges from densely wooded mountains, through undulating countryside with tree and bush covered hills, to open agricultural land. They adapt themselves easily and are, therefore, numerous. Outside the breeding season the adult birds gather together in small groups of five to ten, whereas juveniles prefer flocks of twenty or more immature birds. They are sedentary birds, and never move far from their nest site.

Diet

These parakeets are principally seed eaters; they consume mainly the seeds of grasses, bushes and (eucalyptus) trees, but do not turn their beaks up at berries or other wild fruit, blossom, leaves, nectar, insects and larvae.

Nest-site

Eucalyptus trees are usually chosen for the nest. In aviaries they accept nest-boxes 60cm (2ft) tall, and with a floor size of 20 x 20cm (8 x 8in); the entrance hole should have a diameter of between 8 and 9cm (3 and 3.5in).

Breeding process

The hen lays four to six eggs and incubates them for about twenty days. She leaves the nest for a short time in the early morning and late afternoon to be fed by the cock. It is characteristic of Rosellas that the hen sometimes remains in the box for a considerable time before laying the first egg; in the wild a period of three weeks has been recorded. The cocks will sometimes feed the hen on the nest. The chicks leave the nest about five weeks after hatching and, in the wild, remain with their parents for about the same period before joining a flock of other immature birds. Once they have left they never return to their parents.

General remarks

The Yellow-bellied is the largest of the Rosellas. It is hardy, and the cold does not normally present any problems. It has a quieter character than the other Rosellas.

These birds are probably the oldest and most primitive of the eight species. They are at their most beautiful just after moulting; if the moult was some time ago, the plumage can give a somewhat ruffled impression. It seems that in Tasmania this affects the green birds more than the yellow ones.

Yellow-bellied Rosellas are not often found in aviaries. They deserve more attention, in particular the yellow individuals with smooth and tidy plumages.

PENNANT'S PARAKEET - *Platycercus elegans*

Subspecies
1. *Platycercus elegans elegans*
      Pennant's Parakeet
2. *Platycercus elegans nigrescens*
      (Northern) Pennant's Parakeet
3. *Platycercus elegans melanoptera*
      (Kangaroo Island) Pennant's Parakeet

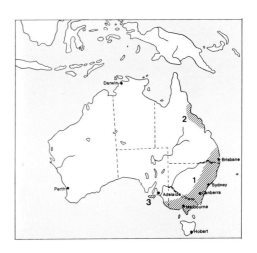

Number 2 is darker red and smaller than number 1. The fledglings of number 2 have a red plumage, whereas a considerable part of the plumage of 1 is green. Number 3 is only found on Kangaroo Island; it has less red than black on its back due to the red edging on each feather being narrower, and this gives it a much darker general appearance.

The subspecies have been frequently crossbred, and, as a result the pure forms are hardly ever found in avicultural collections. They are sometimes vaguely recognizable: larger birds are sometimes a less deep red than smaller ones.

Origin of name
Platycercus: flat or broad tail.
Elegans: elegant.
Nigrescens: becoming black.
Melanoptera: black wing.
Pennant: Thomas Pennant is one of the greatest naturalists ever, and was an important writer on natural history in around 1800.
Dutch: Pennantrosella.
German: Pennantsittich.

Parents and young
It is often difficult to determine the sex of a solitary bird. Cocks and hens look very similar; in fact the only difference is in the size and shape of body, head and beak. In most cases hens are smaller, their heads more rounded, and their beaks less heavy. However, as there is some variation in size within the species, it is best to buy a bird that is still flying round with its brothers and sisters. Under those conditions generally speaking it is possible to pick out a cock or a hen with complete certainty. Make particularly sure that the head of the cock is flattened and angular, and that the beak is broader when viewed from above.

The immature plumage varies greatly, and can be anything from almost completely red to almost completely green. Use the appearance of the parents and the size of the young birds as a guide when making your choice. As the fledglings of the larger subspecies 1 are

31. Pennant's Parakeet; the build, head and beak of the cock (left) is heavier than the hen's

usually green and those of number 2 red, it is sometimes said that the greener the fledglings the bigger they are. However, the fact that one pair can produce young varying from almost green to almost red which nevertheless do not differ in size, is in itself proof that this is by no means true in all cases. The adult plumage develops at about sixteen months old. In the wild Pennant's Parakeets are sexually mature within two years; in aviaries it is becoming more and more common for one-year-old birds to rear young.

Sizes and weights
Lengths: *elegans* 36cm (14in), *nigrescens* 32cm (12.5in), *melanoptera* 34cm (13.5in).
Weights: *elegans* cock 123-169g, *elegans* hen 112-146g, *nigrescens* cock 112-120g.
Ring size: 6mm.

Habitat and habits
As long as the landscape is wooded, Pennant's Parakeets can be found in mountains and hills, and on plains. They are fairly common to very common within their range, and are often to be seen foraging on the ground. They principally inhabit woodland, where they fly around in small flocks.
The cock is the dominant partner.

Diet
These parakeets are not fussy about their food and besides the seeds of grasses, bushes and trees (especially eucalyptuses and acacias), they also eat berries and other fruits, nuts, leaves, blossom, nectar, insects and larvae. However, they are chiefly seed-eaters.

Nest-site
In the wild nests can be anything from one to twenty metres (3 to 66ft) above the ground. In an aviary a box 50 to 60cm (20 to 24in) tall, and with an inside size of 20cm (8 in) square is sufficient. The entrance hole should measure 6 to 7cm (2.5 to 3in).

Breeding process
Adult hens lay four to seven eggs, and the incubation time is about twenty days. In the early morning and late afternoon the hen leaves the nest in order to be fed by the cock, and to defecate.
In the wild the young birds, after leaving their nest, remain with their parents just for a couple of weeks. Sometimes the parents in your aviary are going for a second round. In that case it's recommended to remove the young.

General remarks
Pennant's Parakeets are relatively easy to breed, although particularly during the breeding period adults become more aggressive. Therefore, it is essential that each pair should be housed separately. The cock is rather prone to chasing the hen about.
They are hardy birds which can withstand low temperatures. They are very active and like

32. *Blue Pennant's Parakeet*

to forage about on the floor of the aviary.

The laws of Gloger and Bergmann are very much applicable to Pennant's Parakeets: birds from warmer regions (number 2) are generally smaller than those from colder regions, and the subspecies from the wetter climate (number 2) is darker in colour than that from the drier region (number 1).

As mentioned above some fledglings emerge green from the nest and others red. This is based on observations in the wild. Several years ago in Germany experiments on this phenomenon produced striking results. For a number of years an aviculturist there removed some of the chicks from the nest for a few hours a day, so that they got less food. The young left in the nest were not only fed by their parents, but also given extra food by the keeper. This was repeated with a number of other pairs. The result was that the underfed chicks all fledged red, whereas the chicks in the box all fledged green. Therefore, it seems that diets influence the plumage.

Mutations

There is a fairly common Blue mutation, and also a Yellow, White and Lutino. However, Blue is the only established form, the others are still rare. The Blue Pennant's Parakeet cannot really be regarded as blue, although this mutation is the result of the disappearance of the carotenoid. What was red becomes a greyish colour.

White can be bred from a Blue and a Yellow, and it should be possible to breed an Albino from a Blue and a Lutino. In chapter VII is given how one can go about this.

Lutinos keep their red heads, backs and bellies, but all black and blue feathers become white; their eyes are, of course, red.

The Blue, Yellow and White mutations inherit autosomal recessive; the Lutino probably sex-linked recessive. However, this is not one hundred per cent certain; there are, after all, Lutinos that inherit autosomal recessive.

33. *Pennant's Parakeet; the Yellow mutation*

YELLOW ROSELLA - *Platycercus flaveolus*

Subspecies
None.

Origin of name
Platycercus: flat or broad tail.
Flaveolus: becoming goldish-yellow.
Dutch: strogele rosella.
German: Strohsittich.

Parents and young
Cocks and hens have the same colouring. Many birds have an orangeish-red sheen on their throats and/or breasts; this is usually more noticeable on hens than on cocks.
Furthermore there is a slight difference in size. The head and beak of the cock is heavier, and the head is flatter and more angular; the hen has a rounder head, and is often slightly smaller. Cocks have no wing bar, and usually neither do hens. As the birds get older the colours become deeper.
Immature birds have olive green backs and yellowish-green bellies. Their full adult plumage appears with the first complete moult at an age of twelve to sixteen months. At two years old they are, generally speaking, sexually mature.

Sizes and weights
Length: 34cm (13.5in).
Weights: cock 110-135g, hen 105-117g.
Ring size: 6mm.

Habitat and habits
The Yellow Rosella has only a very limited distribution range consisting mainly of the Murray and Murrumbidgee Rivers and their tributaries, where they are, however, common. They have a preference for Red River Eucalyptuses, in which they search for their food in the outside branches either in pairs or in small groups.
For the rest their habits are the same as those of the Pennant's Parakeet.

Diet
The seeds of the above mentioned Red River Eucalyptus are of importance; they also eat the seeds of other trees, grasses and bushes, blossom, nectar, leaves, nuts, berries and other wild fruit, insects and larvae.

34. Yellow Rosella; a cock missing the read on the breast

Nest-site
The nest is situated high above the ground, usually in a tree standing either in or alongside water. In aviaries a box measuring 60 x 20 x 20cm (24 x 8 x 8in) is suitable. The diameter of the entrance hole should be 6 to 7cm (2.5 to 3in).

Breeding process
The hen lays four to six eggs, which she then incubates for about twenty days. She leaves the nest for a short time in the early morning and late afternoon to be fed and to defecate. After about five weeks the chicks have fledged; they remain with their parents for some time, but not for very long. A second clutch is very occasionally laid; if this does occur it is advisable to separate the young birds from their parents.

General remarks
Aviculturists have a preference for birds without the orange-red sheen on their throat and/or breast, like the bird in the photograph.
However, birds with this 'defect' are also found in the wild and it is, of course, not a disaster as long as it is slightly visible. It is purely a matter of taste; the presence of red on a bird says nothing about the quality. The Yellow Rosella has a lot in common with the Pennant's Parakeet and the Adelaide Rosella.

35. *Adelaide Rosella; the reddish-brown of these species varies greatly*

136

ADELAIDE ROSELLA - *Platycercus adelaidae*

Subspecies

1. *Platycercus adelaidae adelaidae*
   Adelaide Rosella
2. *Platycercus adelaidae subadelaidae*
   Adelaide Rosella

The predominant reddish-brown number 1 gives it a similar appearance to the Pennant's Parakeet; number 2 is more orange-yellow and, therefore, looks more like the Yellow Rosella.

In Australia the two subspecies are separated from each other by a strip of land about fifty to sixty kilometres wide.

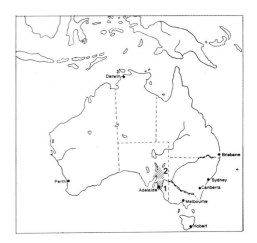

Origin of name

Platycercus: flat or broad tail.
Adelaidae: after the town of Adelaide in southern Australia.
Dutch: Adelaiderosella.
German: Adelaidesittich.

Parents and young

The colouring of adult birds is very variable and there are virtually no two alike. They show various combinations of brownish and yellowish tints, and as in captivity the two subspecies have been indiscriminately crossbred all manner of hybrids are found in collections.

The differences between cocks and hens are the same as for Pennant's Parakeet and the Yellow Rosella: the cock is more heavily-built and has a larger head and beak. He has no wing bar and usually the hen hasn't one either.

Young birds are more of an ashy green, and they may have the odd reddish-brown feather. They develop their adult plumage after about sixteen months, and six months later they are ready to breed. For the first few years the colour of the plumage becomes gradually deeper.

Sizes and weights

Length: 35cm (14in).
Weights: cock 112-165g, hen 100-160g.
Ring size: 6mm.

Habitat and habits

These parakeets inhabit an area about the size of Greater London around the town of

137

Adelaide in southern Australia. They are not very particular in their choice of habitat and can be found in wooded valleys, in open woods, in trees lining roads and watercourses, and on agricultural land. They are not great travellers and usually remain in the same surroundings.

Diet
Despite their preference for the seeds of eucalyptuses they do eat the seeds of other trees, of bushes and grasses; also insects and larvae, blossom, leaves, nectar, berries and other wild fruits, and nuts.

Nest-site
The choice of nest-site is very similar to that of the Pennant's Parakeet and the Yellow Rosella. They often pick out the taller trees. The aviculturist should use a box measuring 60 x 20 x 20cm (24 x 8 x 8in) with an 6 to 7cm (2.5 to 3in) entrance hole.

Breeding process
The four to six eggs are incubated for about twenty days. The chicks fledge about thirty-five days after hatching and then remain with their parents for several weeks. For the rest the same applies as for the Pennant's Parakeet and the Yellow Rosella.

General remarks
Although most experts regard the Pennant's Parakeet, and the Yellow and Adelaide Rosellas as separate subspecies, there are those who claim that the Adelaide is nothing more than a cross between the Yellow and the Pennant. They do indeed look somewhere between the two, and a cross between a Yellow Rosella and a Pennant's Parakeet has a very similar appearance. The three are in any case very closely related to each other.
Our climate presents no problems for these birds. Their aggressive nature should be taken into account, particularly in the breeding season; this also applies to the cock's aggression towards his mate.

Mutations
A Lutino mutation of this Rosella is known to exist. It has been observed in the wild, and a few aviculturists in Australia have this bird in their collection. It cannot be found in Europe as yet.
It seems that the mode of inheritance is autosomal recessive.

36. *Pennant's Parakeet; immature (above left)*
37. *Yellow Rosella; immature (above right)*
38. *Adelaide Rosella; immature (below right)*
These photographs show clearly that these young birds are closely related

139

39. Eastern Rosella; the colouring of the cock (right) is deeper than the hen's

EASTERN ROSELLA - *Platycercus eximius*

Subspecies

1. *Platycercus eximius eximius*
                          Eastern Rosella
2. *Platycerus eximius cecilae*
                          Golden-mantled Rosella
3. *Platycerus eximius diemenensis*
                          Tasmanian Rosella

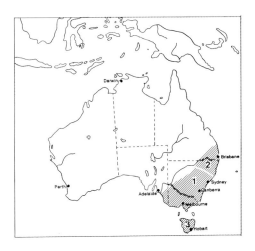

The heads and breasts of particularly the cocks of number 2 are darker red than number 1; the feathers on the backs of number 2 are black with goldish-yellow edging, and those of number 1 black with yellowish-green; the rumps of number 2 are bluish-green and of number 1 clear pale green. The Golden-mantled Rosella, therefore, gives a much more colourful impression.

Number 3 looks similar to number 1, but the white cheek patches are larger, the red is darker, and the rump is light blue. It is only found in Tasmania.

Origin of name

Platycercus: flat or broad tail.
Eximius: excellent, outstanding.
Cecilae: after Cecilia, a relation of Gregory M. Mathews.
Diemenensis: from van Diemensland, the former name for Tasmania.
Rosella: probably after Rose Hill, near Sydney.
Dutch: rosella (*P. e. cecilae*: prachtrosella).
German: Rosellasittich.

Parents and young

Cocks are more brightly coloured than hens; the red of their head and breast is particularly eye-catching. The red patch on the breast is not always rounded, but in many cases runs down into a V-shape. This is typical of this species. Cocks have no wing bar, but hens often do. Finally, hens do have a slighter build.

The pure forms of the subspecies are hardly ever found in aviaries; they have been extensively crossbred. Therefore, aviculturists who wish to keep these birds would do well to concentrate on just one of the subspecies, and to try to breed as pure a form as possible. Number 2 already enjoys more attention in this respect than either of the others.

Immature birds look very similar to the hen, but have less red and more green. Immature hens are paler again than immature cocks, and in most cases the latter have a little more red. Young birds develop their plumage in a little more than a year, and they often start breeding when they are nearly a year old.

141

40. *Rosella; Red or Opaline mutation*

It is sometimes said that hens keep the yellow patches on the head longer than cocks, and it seems to be a characteristic of Golden-mantled Rosellas that some hens never lose these patches.

Sizes and weights
Length: 31cm (12in).
Weights: cock 97-120g, hen 90g.
Ring size: 5.4mm.

Habitat and habits
Eastern Rosellas are found in wooded savannahs, open woodland, trees lining watercourses and around fields of cereals. They also appear in orchards, parks and gardens, and in the outskirts of towns and villages. To a certain extent they profit by a cultured landscape, and they are found in the greater parts of the most fertile regions in southeast Australia.
Outside the breeding season they gather into small groups, which can sometimes grow into flocks of a hundred or more birds. They are sedentary birds, and spend a lot of time on the ground foraging.
Cocks can be extremely aggressive. I myself had a cock for a long time which hens found impossible to live with; they often fled into the nest box in fright. He chased them around so much that breeding was out of the question.

Diet
Just as other Rosellas these birds are especially keen on the seeds of trees (particularly eucalyptuses and acacias), bushes, and grasses, but they also eat berries and other wild fruit, nuts, leaves and other greenery, blossom, nectar, insects and larvae.

Nest-site
Somebody in Australia has carried out a study into more than thirty nest-sites. He came to the conclusion that these Rosellas do not have a clear preference: he found nests in both sloping and upright branches and trunks, long and short tunnels, and small and large entrance holes. One nest, for example, was situated in a fallen tree with a trunk the diameter of a tennis ball and eggs were within 35cm of the opening. Some entrance holes were the size of dinner plates, and some were so small that the birds could only just squeeze through.
The average size for a nest-box in the aviary is 50 x 20 x 20cm (20 x 8 x 8in), with a 6cm (2.5in) diameter entrance hole.

Breeding process
The number of eggs laid by this species varies rather, and may number four to nine. The incubating time is about twenty days. During this period the hen leaves the box two or three times a day in order to eat, be fed by the cock, and to defecate. The cock sometimes feeds the hen on the nest.
Newly-hatched chicks are fed by the hen for the first ten days, and later on the cock also

41. Rosella; Isabel hen

does his share of the work. The chicks fledge at about five weeks. In the wild they then remain with their parents for many weeks.

Birds in aviaries sometimes start laying as early as February, and it is not unusual for them to rear two clutches. In the case of a second clutch it is advisable to remove the young birds from the parents.

General remarks

Eastern Rosellas are excellent birds for the inexperienced birdkeeper; they are not expensive, are eager breeders and, furthermore, are exceptionally beautiful parakeets. The only disadvantage is that they can be rather aggressive. To show these birds at their best the flight should be three to four metres (10 to 13ft) long. It is a pity that so few pure bred birds exist; however, a lot can be achieved by selecting breeding stock carefully.

I came across a case in which the hen died after the eggs had hatched and the cock reared the five chicks on his own.

Rosellas are good examples for Gloger's Law, described in the introduction to this chapter: the Golden-mantled Rosella is found in the drier regions and the Eastern Rosella in the wetter.

Mutations

The mutations bred so far are Lutino, White-winged, Dilute, Isabel and Red.

The Lutino Rosella was reported in Australia years ago, but it is not known what further developments have taken place.

The White-winged appeared in Belgium, and is now bred with on a reasonable scale. This bird has a white tail, light-coloured legs, a goldish-yellow back with little black, less red on the head and a yellow stripe above the eye. The mode of inheritance is dominant.

The Isabel and the Dilute are very similar; the photograph shows an Isabel hen. This bird has brownish tints, particularly on the flight feathers, whereas the Dilute mutation tends to be grey, principally on the flight feathers. The Isabel inherits sex-linked recessive, and the Dilute autosomal recessive.

The Red Rosella is a very unusual looking bird: the entire belly and breast are a uniform red, as are partly the feathers on the back. The breast feathers have a white base, which is visible when the feathers are fluffed up. The hen has a lighter tail than the cock; both sexes retain a white stripe on the underside of the wing, but the hens's is broader.

The Red Rosella is actually an Opaline mutation. The mode of inheritance is sex-linked recessive.

42. Blue-cheeked Rosella; cock and hen. The relationship to the Mealy Rosella is clearly visible

BLUE-CHEEKED ROSELLA
Platycercus adscitus adscitus

Subspecies
1. *Platycercus adscitus adscitus*
                Blue-cheeked Rosella
2. *Platycercus adscitus palliceps*
        Mealy Rosella, Pale-headed Rosella
The Mealy Rosella is dealt with in the next description. The photographs clearly show the differences. The Blue-cheeked has greenish-yellow edging on the mantle feathers, and the Mealy is yellower.
Furthermore, the rump of number 1 is greenish-yellow and that of number 2 bluish. The sides of the Blue-cheeks' belly are bluer; this is connected with its warmer and wetter distribution range (Gloger's Law).

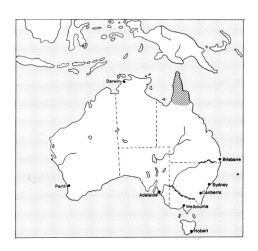

Origin of name
Platycercus: flat or broad tail.
Adscitus: adopted, new.
Dutch: blauwwangrosella.
German: Blauwangenrosella.

Parents and young
There is no clear difference between cocks and hens. The main difference is the same as for most other Rosellas: cocks are more heavily-built, and have larger heads and beaks. Cocks have no wing bar, but hens often do. The general plumage of young birds is duller than the adults', and they often have a few grey and red feathers on their heads. The full adult plumage appears after the first total moult at an age of about sixteen months. They are able to breed for the first time at the end of their second year.

Sizes and weights
Length: 30cm (12in).
Weights: cock 100-105g.
Ring size: 6mm.

Habitat and habits
Blue-cheeked Rosellas are mainly found in the tropical and subtropical regions of

northeastern Australia. They are birds of the lowland areas, where they inhabit the lightly-wooded, more open land. They live in pairs or in small groups, and remain in the same area for most of the time. They often search on the ground for food. Their distribution range is wetter and warmer than the Mealy Rosella's; birds from such regions are more colourful than subspecies from cooler and drier regions.

The Blue-cheeked is possibly the most aggressive of all the rosellas.

Diet

The eating habits of the Blue-cheeked Rosellas do not differ from that of other Australian Parakeets: seeds of grasses, bushes and trees, fruit, nuts, blossom, nectar, leafbuds, insects and larvae. As they live in tropical and subtropical regions there is a huge food supply.

Nest-site

Nests are normally found in eucalyptus trees near water. In the aviary a nest-box should be supplied with a height of 50cm (20in), and a floor size of 20 x 20cm (8 x 8in). An entrance hole with a diameter of 6cm (2.5in) is sufficient.

Breeding process

After choosing a nest-site the hen lays four to seven eggs, which she then incubates for about twenty days. The hen receives most of her food from the cock, and after the eggs have hatched he also does his share in rearing the young. The young birds can be separated from their parents about three weeks after they have fledged. There is often only one clutch.

General remarks

Blue-cheeked Rosellas are less common than Mealy Rosellas. Many aviculturists have probably never seen them in a pure form. It is extremely desirable for the two subspecies to survive in pure forms, and crossbreeding should be avoided at all times. The specific characteristics and colouring of both must be preserved.

These parakeets bathe a good deal. It seems that they are less hardy than the other Australian parakeets. They are fairly critical in their choice of mate.

Of the birds now present in avicultural collections only a small number are pure-bred. These birds are treated with the greatest care, so there is some hope that the size of the breeding stock will slowly increase.

MEALY ROSELLA - *Platycercus adscitus palliceps*

Subspecies
The Mealy Rosella is a subspecies of the Blue-cheeked Rosella previously described. The Mealy is much better known. Its back is yellow as opposed to the Blue-cheek's greenish-yellow; it also has a bluish rump, whereas the Blue-cheek's is greenish-yellow. The Mealy is slightly larger.

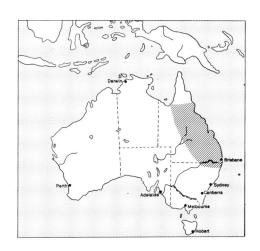

Origin of name
Platycercus: flat or broad tail.
Adscitus: adopted, new.
Palliceps: pale head.
Dutch: bleekkoprosella.
German: Blasskopfrosella.

Parents and young
The plumage of the Mealy Rosella is very variable; big differences are sometimes found among birds of this subspecies. This is particularly noticeable on the back (from goldish-yellow to greenish-yellow) and on the belly (from light to dark blue). The head and beak of the cocks are heavier than the hen's; he may also be more brightly-coloured, but it is very difficult to distinguish the cocks from the hens. Adult cocks have no wing stripe, and hens often do.
The colours of immature birds are duller, and in many cases red feathers are visible on the head. These disappear when the birds are full-grown. The full adult plumage appears after the first total moult at an age of about sixteen months. Young birds start breeding six months after this moult.

Sizes and weights
Length: 32cm (12.5in).
Weights: cock 131g, hen 112g.
Ring size: 6mm.

Habitat and habits
In this respect the Mealy Rosella shows a certain similarity to the Blue-cheeked Rosella; it has a preference for lightly-wooded grassland and savannah, trees lining watercourses, and dry regions with bushy vegetation.
They are found in more southerly areas than the Blue-cheeks, where it is drier and colder. They are generally encountered foraging on the ground in pairs or in small groups. They

43. *Mealy Rosella; a cock with a splendid goldish-yellow back*

are sedentary. Mealy Rosellas can be very aggressive, particularly in the breeding season.

Diet
Their diet consists of a variety of herb and grass seeds; they also eat berries and other wild fruit, nuts, leafbuds, blossom, nectar, insects and larvae, and the seeds of bushes and trees.

Nest-site
In the wild the hen selects a suitable cavity which is usually in a eucalyptus tree near water.
In an aviary a nest-box measuring 50 x 20 x 20cm (20 x 8 x 8in) should be made available to her.

Breeding process
A clutch numbers four to seven eggs, and the incubation time is about twenty days. The hen starts sitting after laying the second or third egg, and the chicks leave the nest about five weeks after hatching. When the chicks are a few days old the cock helps the hen to feed them. In the wild the young birds remain with their parents for some time. This is not possible in an aviary as the cock may well become rather aggressive.
Usually, only one clutch is reared each year.

General remarks
Mealy Rosellas are hardy aviary birds which, as long as they are provided with some shelter, have no trouble getting through our winters.
They are not the easiest birds to breed; they are fairly critical in their choice of mate, and this means that the immediate production of young is far from guaranteed. A certain amount of patience is required, and in some cases birds may have to be substituted.
The Mealy Rosella is also called the Pale-headed Rosella.

Mutations
A, still extremely rare, Dilute mutation exists; it is a slightly lighter form than the normal bird.

44. Brown's Parakeet; cock (left) and hen (right)

BROWN'S PARAKEET - *Platycercus venustus*

Subspecies
None.

Origin of name
Platycercus: flat or broad tail.
Venustus: after Venus, the Roman goddess of love.
Brown: this parakeet was discovered by the British biologist Robert Brown (1773-1858), who explored the Australian coast on board the ship the Investigator from 1802 to 1805.
Dutch: Brownrosella.
German: Brownssittich.

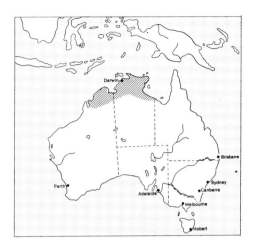

Parents and young
It is difficult to tell the cocks from the hens of this species. Although hens are sometimes slightly smaller and have rounder heads, this is not true in all cases. Neither does the wing stripe give any certainty: cocks lack it and usually the hens as well. The heads of cocks are sometimes deeper black.
Immature birds look very similar to adults, but they are slightly duller, and may have a few red feathers on their heads. After twelve to fifteen months their adult plumage has developed, and they are sexually mature after two years.

Sizes and weights
Length: 28cm (11in).
Weights: cock 92-112g, hen 88 -92g.
Ring size: 5.4mm.

Habitat and habits
Brown's Parakeets are found in northern Australia in open woodland, particularly near rivers and other watercourses. Their distribution is not even, in some places they are common and in others rare. They live in pairs or in groups of six to eight in the tops of trees or on the ground searching for food.
In the wild these parakeets are very shy and they avoid inhabited areas. They are not sedentary, but travel about.

Diet
These parakeets eat the seeds of grasses, acacias and eucalyptuses, but also blossom,

nectar, insects and larvae. They eat more insects than most other Rosellas and have a taste for various species of beetles and grubs.

Nest-site

The chicks are reared in cavities in eucalyptuses in the vicinity of water. A 50 to 60cm (20 to 24in) high nest-box, with a 20cm (8 in) square floor can be used in an aviary. The entrance hole should measure 5.5cm (2.25in).

Breeding process

This species produces smaller clutches than other Rosellas; the number of eggs varies from two to four, and sometimes five. The incubation time is about twenty days, and during this period the cock feeds his mate. He continues to do this for a time after the eggs have hatched. The chicks fledge after about five weeks and in the wild they remain with their parents for quite some time. On the odd occasion a second clutch is laid, it is advisable to rehouse the young birds. You must in any case watch for signs of the cock behaving aggressively towards his offspring, and then take the same measures if necessary.

Brown's Parakeets have not yet adjusted to the West European climate and to the changing of the seasons. This means that they start breeding at the end of the summer. The incubation period, therefore, is during the autumn, and this demands extra care and attention from the birdkeeper. As the number of daylight hours decreases, the keeper must see to it that there is sufficient time for the feeding of the chicks; if necessary artificial lighting must be arranged. Furthermore, it is advisable to keep an eye on the temperature; the young birds are much more sensitive to hypothermia in our chilly, damp autumn than in tropical northern Australia.

General remarks

Brown's Parakeets are not easy birds to breed, and only suitable for the experienced aviculturist. The biggest problem is establishing a good breeding pair, as they are exceptionally particular in their choice of partner. Furthermore, cocks can be very aggressive towards hens, and they can even go so far as to kill them. The birdkeeper must, therefore, constantly keep an eye on the birds' behaviour.

A spacious aviary with plenty of places of refuge is not out of the way for these parakeets, and a length of five metres (16ft 6in) is no luxury.

Clutches of unfertilized eggs are fairly common, and the birds are quite easily affected by disturbances.

Finally, an eye should be kept on the weather. It is understandable that these birds from the tropics should be susceptible to cold. The birdkeeper must be watchful during hard frosts, and it is advisable to have some form of heating at hand.

STANLEY PARAKEET - *Platycercus icterotis*

Subspecies

1. *Platycercus icterotis icterotis*
Stanley Parakeet
2. *Platycercus ictorotis xanthogenys*
(Yellow-cheeked) Stanley Parakeet

The differences between these two can be found on the back, mantle and rump. The feathers on the back and mantle of number 1 have a black centre and a green edging which has a variable red sheen; the cheek patches are yellow and the rump is green. The feathers on the back of number 2 have a black centre and a red edging which can have a yellow sheen; the cheek patches are pale yellow and the rump is greyish-green. Probably neither species

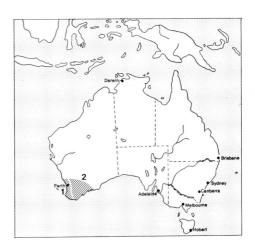

can be found in avicultural collections in their pure form. The majority of birdkeepers think a Stanley is a Stanley, and pay little or no attention to the differences mentioned.

Origin of name

Platycercus: flat or broad tail.
Icterotis: yellow ear.
Xanthogenys: yellow cheek.
Stanley: Edward Smith Stanley, the thirteenth Count of Derby (1775-1851), who built up one of the largest and most beautiful collections of animals and birds in Europe at his country home.
Dutch: Stanleyrosella.
German: Stanleysittich.

Parents and young

The Stanley Parakeet is the only Rosella with a clear difference between the cock and the hen. The belly and breast of the cock is solid red, whereas the hen's is spotted with green. The yellow cheek patch of the cock almost reaches the eye, whereas the hen's stops short of it. Finally, the cock lacks the wing stripe which the hen possesses.
Immature birds are principally green and have no or only faint cheek patches. After the first partial moult in autumn they become more colourful, and it is then easier to tell the sexes apart, as the cocks are then more brightly-coloured. The full adult plumage appears after about fourteen months. Young birds are able to reproduce after only a year.

45. *Stanley Parakeet: the only Rosella with a clear difference between the cocks and hens*

Sizes and weights
Length: 27cm (10.5in).
Weights: cock 59-80g, hen 52-71g.
Ring size: 5.4mm.

Habitat and habits
The Stanley Parakeet is the only Rosella which is found in southwestern Australia, where it lives in the wettest part. It has a preference for lightly-wooded areas: open woodland; grassland; trees around fields of cereals, and along roads and watercourses; and in orchards. This parakeet is fairly adaptable and profits from cultivated land, and consequently can be regarded as fairly common.
Stanleys roam around in pairs or in family groups, and are seldom seen in larger flocks, even outside the breeding season.
They are the least aggressive of all the rosellas.

Diet
Their staple diet consists of the seeds of grasses and herb-like plants, which they often search for on the ground. In addition they eat berries and other fruit, blossom, nectar, leafbuds, insects and larvae.

Nest-site
The hen usually selects a eucalyptus tree.
In the aviary she will be satisfied with a nest-box 50cm (20in) tall, with a floor measuring 18 x 18cm (7 x 7in), and an entrance hole with a diameter of 5 to 6cm (2 to 2.5in).

Breeding process
The clutch numbers four to seven eggs, which the hen incubates for nineteen to twenty days. She leaves the nest in the early morning and late afternoon to eat and to be fed by the cock. He feeds her on the nest as well, also when the chicks have hatched. After a few days he also helps to provide the chicks with food. They usually leave the nest after about five weeks like the chicks of other Rosellas, but occasionally this happens earlier.
Some pairs produce a second clutch; if this occurs it is advisable to remove the young birds.

General remarks
Stanley Parakeets have lived completely isolated from all other species of Rosella for a very long time, and this gives them a special position within the group. They are distinguishable by their smaller size, the difference between cocks and hens, their tolerant nature, and the immature birds' lack of cheek patches. For this reason they are considered by some experts to be an intermediate form between the genuses Platycercus (Rosellas) and Psephotus (Red-rumps etc.), also because their flight is similar to the latter's.
Just as other rosellas Stanleys like to bathe. They easily withstand our climate, and need a flight at least three metres (10ft) long. They are admirably suitable for the inexperienced birdkeeper.
It would be a good thing if the existence of the two subspecies were taken into account when forming breeding pairs, and if an attempt were made to produce pure-bred birds, so that in the future we will be able to show both forms.

46. Stanley Parakeet; after a short time some difference between the sexes of immature birds is already visible

Genus *Psephotus*

Generally speaking any birdkeeper is able to see for himself that the various species belonging to the same genus are related. However, although this is true for most genuses, the relationship is much less obvious within the *Psephotus* group. This comprises five species and an extra four subspecies, which can be divided into three distinguishable groups:

1. the Red-rumped Parakeet and the Many-coloured Parakeet. These are known to all birdkeepers; they are birds which anybody is able to keep. There is a striking difference between cocks and hens. Both nest in hollow trunks or branches;

2. the Golden-shouldered Parakeet, the Hooded Parakeet and the Paradise Parakeet. The cocks and hens of this group also look different. They are birds for the experienced aviculturist. In the wild these birds do not nest in hollow trees, but in cavities in termite hills which they dig out themselves. The Paradise Parakeet is probably extinct and is not found in avicultural collections. This species is, therefore, not further dealt with.
    Whereas the colouring of the first group is principally green, with this it is particularly the handsome blue on the bellies of the cocks that is striking;

3. the Yellow-vented Blue-bonnet, the Red-vented Blue-bonnet and the Naretha Blue-bonnet. The colouring of these birds is basically greyish-brown. There is no great difference between cocks and hens: hens are slightly smaller and a little more soberly coloured. They nest in hollow trunks or branches. Their most striking characteristic is the nodding action of the head.

There are a few other similarities between these species which are worth mentioning. The Golden-shouldered, the Hooded, and the Blue-bonnet are able to raise their crown feathers into a small crest; they do this particularly when alarmed or excited during the courtship display. Further, the Blue-bonnet, and to a lesser extent the Hooded, jump stiff-legged up and down. Some birds shake their tails when excited or during courtship; Hoodeds do this with a closed tail, Red-rumps, Many-coloureds and Blue-bonnets with their tails fanned.

The bond between breeding pairs of this genus is stronger than that of other Australian parakeets. This is, among other things, noticeable by the elaborate way in which they preen each other.
Another point is that they can be extremely aggressive, particularly the Red-rumps and the Blue-bonnets.
They are birds of Australia's drier regions.

genus	species	subspecies	
Psephotus	*haematonotus*	*haematonotus*	1. Red-rumped Parakeet
"	"	*caeruleus*	2. (Pale) Red-rumped Parakeet
"	*varius*	-	3. Many-coloured Parakeet
"	*haematogaster*	*haematogaster*	4. Yellow-vented Blue-bonnet
"	"	*haematorrhous*	5. Red-vented Blue-bonnet
"	"	*pallescens*	6. (Pale) Yellow-vented Blue-Bonnet
"	"	*narethae*	7. Naretha Blue-bonnet
"	*chrysopterygius*	*chrysopterygius*	8. Golden-shouldered Parakeet
"	"	*dissimilis*	9. Hooded Parakeet
"	*pulcherrimus*		10. Paradise Parakeet

RED-RUMPED PARAKEET - *Psephotus haematonotus*

Subspecies
1. *Psephotus haematonotus haematonotus*
                    Red-rumped Parakeet
2. *Psephotus haematonotus caeruleus*
                    (Pale) Red-rumped Parakeet
The green of number 2 is paler and bluer, particularly on the mantle and back; the rump is pale orange-red. The hen is also slightly paler. Birds in aviaries here are most similar to number 1.

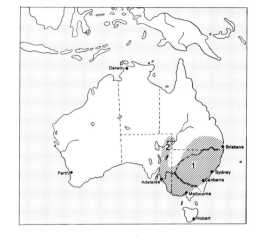

Origin of name
Psephotus: inlaid with mosaic.
Haematonotus: bloody back.
Caeruleus: dark blue.
Dutch: roodrugparkiet.
German: Singsittich.

Parents and young
The difference between cocks and hens is self-evident. Cock chicks can be distinguished even in the nest: they soon have red feathers on their rumps and greener feathers on their heads. On fledging young birds are duller than their parents, however, after three or four months they have already developed their adult plumage. Birds born here are already sexually mature within a year.

Sizes and weights
Length: 27cm (10.5in).
Weights: cock 68-70g, hen 54-65g.
Ring size: 5mm.

Habitat and habits
Red-rumped Parakeets are not very particular and can be found in many different types of country, as long as it contains trees; the only habitat they really avoid is dense woodland. They even come into parks and gardens and, as they benifit from cultured land, they have remained common birds. The subspecies caeruleus is more often found in the real desert regions, where the average rainfall is less than 10cm (4in) a year. Red-rumps live in pairs or small groups during the breeding season, and in flocks of a hundred or more outside it; although within these flocks it seems that the bond between mates remains.
Shortly after sunrise they drink, and then they leave for the feeding grounds, where they remain until dusk. They spend a lot of time on the ground foraging for grass seeds. They rest during the middle of the day.

161

47. Red-rumped Parakeet; the cock shows why this species bears this name. His breast is green, and his belly yellow

Diet
These parakeets chiefly eat the seeds of grasses, herb-like plants, and bushes such as acacias, and, therefore, are often seen on the ground. It seems that they rarely eat berries or other fruit, but they do consume a lot of green food.

Nest-site
Nests are normally found in eucalyptus trees growing near water. A number of nests are sometimes found in the same area.
Birds in aviaries are not too particular; they usually find a box 40cm (16in) high, and 15cm (6in) square acceptable. The entrance hole should have a diameter of 5 to 6cm (2 to 2.5in).

Breeding process
Four to six eggs are laid, which are incubated by the hen for about nineteen days. During this period the cock provides her with most of her food, and she usually leaves the box to be fed. When the chicks have hatched they are fed by the hen at first, but once their feathers start to appear the cock joins in. In the wild after the chicks have fledged, at a good four weeks old, the parents and young join one of the larger flocks. This is not possible in an aviary, and as a result of the limited space, the cock sometimes starts chasing his sons around. This can get so bad that either the father or one of the young has to be removed. There is very often a second clutch; sometimes even followed by a third.

General remarks
Many birdkeepers began their hobby by purchasing a pair of Red-rumped Parakeets. They are the ideal birds for the beginner: they are attractive. hardy, adaptable, and they are reasonably easy to breed. Their only fault is that they can be aggressive, particularly in the breeding season. That means that each pair must be housed separately. Another advantage

48. Red-rumped Parakeet: Blue cock and hen   *49. Red-rumped Parakeet: Blue cock and White hen*

50. Red-rumped Parakeet; the red has disappeared from the rump of the cock (left) of this Olive-Pied mutation. The difference in the yellow does not always distinguish the cocks from the hens

of these birds is that they make excellent foster parents, sometimes even for non-Australian parakeets. However, it is better not to entrust them with the eggs of too large a species. An aviary three metres (10ft) long is suitable. Red-rumps make an exceptionally pleasant whistling noise. It is not known in Germany as the "Singing Parakeet" for nothing.

Mutations

Various mutations have seen the light of day. It seems that in Australia one can find the Lutino, Cinnamon, Fallow, Blue, and Pastel-Blue. As far as I know not all of these are on show here, but a number are. The best known is the so-called Yellow Red-rump, which has featured in avicultural collections for many years. The name is not entirely accurate, as it is in fact a Cinnamon mutation, but it will probably continue to be used. One of the latest additions is the Olive-Pied Red-rump. Its most striking feature is the total lack of red on the cock's rump. The amount of yellow is rather variable, but is not a clear indication as to the sex of the birds; there is no obvious difference between cocks and hens. Futher, there is the White Red-rump, the result of the combination Yellow (Cinnamon) x (Dilute) Blue. As these colours are not entirely pure, the white mutation is not pure white either. This mutation can only be bred from the offspring of split birds. Finally, the Yellow Red-rump with red eyes should be mentioned. This bird is not pure yellow like a Lutino, but the colouring is more Dilute.
The Cinnamon and Fallow Red-rumps inherit sex-linked recessive, the (Dilute-)Blue, Lutino, and the Olive-Pied have the autosomal recessive mode of inheritance.

51. Red-rumped Parakeet: Yellow or Cinnamon mutation

165

52. Many-coloured Parakeet; hen and cock

MANY-COLOURED PARAKEET - *Psephotus varius*

Subspecies
None.

Origin of name
Psephotus: inlaid with mosaic.
Varius: pied, many coloured.
Dutch: veelkleurenparkiet.
German: Vielfarbensittich.

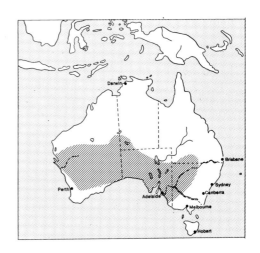

Parents and young
The photograph shows the difference between cock and hen clearly enough; only the red patch on the head of the cock is not visible.
The colouring is rather variable, and one bird can look much more handsome than another, particularly when cocks are involved. The red patch on the lower belly is especially variable, and aviculturists prefer this to be as big and bright as possible. Compared to the Red-rumped Parakeet the hen has a yellowish head and a reddish-brown wing bar. The adult male lacks this wing bar.
The chicks can be sexed while still in the nest: cocks are larger than hens, however, at first they have little or no red on their lower belly. The young birds develop their adult plumage after six months, and they start breeding at one year old.

Sizes and weights
Length: 28cm (11in).
Weights: cock 56-65g, hen 53-70g.
Ring size: 5mm.

Habitat and habits
The Many-coloured Parakeet show a preference for areas with little rainfall; they sometimes have to lead a nomadic existence in search of water. They avoid towns and villages, and also large trees and dense woods. They sometimes sit in tall eucalyptus trees along watercourses, and are often found in the so-called mulga areas, which is why Australians call the Many-coloured the Mulga Parrot: mulga is a species of acacia. It will be clear that they are found in drier areas than the Red-rumped Parakeet. They are fairly common within these areas but they are not numerous anywhere.
Unlike the Red-rumped they rarely form large flocks, although occasionally they are found in fairly large numbers in feeding and watering places. However, they are normally seen on the ground in pairs or in family groups searching for food.

Diet

Many-coloured Parakeets are mainly dependent upon the seeds of grasses, plants, bushes and trees for their food, and are often observed eating the seeds of the mulga, Acacia aneura. They also eat various sorts of green food, insects and larvae.

Nest-site

They have no preference for any particular nest cavity, and they are found at various heights. However, they often choose a tree close to a river or other watercourse.

In an aviary they are quite content with a nest box with a height of 45cm (18in), and a floor measuring 15 x 15cm (6 x 6in); the diameter of the entrance hole should be 5 to 6cm (2 to 2.5in).

Breeding process

An average clutch numbers four to seven eggs. These may be laid fairly early; sometimes even in February. The incubation time is about twenty days, and the chicks remain in the nest-box for a little under five weeks.

While the hen is incubating the cock occasionally tempts her out of the box in order to feed her or to get her to eat. He sometimes enters the box himself with food. For the first few days the chicks are fed by the hen alone, but after a week the cock does his share. Hens sometimes leave young chicks alone in the box for longer periods; this can cause problems, particularly if the weather is cold, as the chicks are not able to keep themselves warm.

In the wild the offspring remain with their parents after they have fledged, and the birds then roam around in family groups until the beginning of the next breeding season. There is less chance of this being possible in an aviary as the cock may become aggressive towards his sons. Besides, a second clutch is sometimes laid.

During the breeding season Many-coloured Parakeets tend to start fights with other birds, so they should always have an aviary to themselves.

General remarks

As mentioned above, the name Mulga Parrot refers to a tree, the *Acacia aneura*, which is very common in the drier areas of the interior of Australia and which holds a great attraction for the Many-coloured Parakeet.

In aviaries they spend quite a lot of time foraging around on the floor. They need a space at least three metres (10ft) long in which to fly.

Our climate presents no problems for these birds, and they are admirably suitable for the inexperienced birdkeeper.

YELLOW-VENTED BLUE-BONNET
Psephotus haematogaster haematogaster

Subspecies

1. *Psephotus haematogaster*
   haematogaster
   Yellow-vented Blue-bonnet
2. *Psephotus haematogaster*
   haematorrhous
   Red-vented Blue-bonnet
3. *Psephotus haematogaster pallescens*
   (Pale) Yellow-vented Blue-bonnet
4. *Psephotus haematogaster narethae*
   Naretha Blue-bonnet

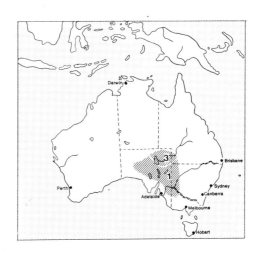

Number 1 has yellow undertail-coverts, and olive on its wings; number 2 has red undertail-coverts, and reddish-brown instead of olive on its wings; number 3 looks similar to number 1 but the plumage is visibly paler, particularly the breast and back; number 4 is smaller and is the only one without any red on its belly, although the undertail-coverts are red.

Numbers 2 and 4 are dealt with separately later; I restrict myself here to numbers 1 and 3; pure-bred birds of the latter species are not to be found in avicultural collections, although a certain amount of colour variation is found.

Origin of name

Psephotus: inlaid with mosaic.
Haematogaster: blood-red belly.
Pallescens: becoming pale.
Yellow-vented: with a yellow rectum; vent = anus.
Dutch: yellow-vented blue-bonnet.
German: Gelbsteissittich.

Parents and young

Cocks and hens are very alike; however, hens have a little less red on their bellies, the blue on their heads is slightly duller and a little less extensive, and their beaks are a shade smaller. Cocks have no wing bar, whereas hens usually do.

The colouring of immature birds is slightly duller, and they have less red on their bellies. They have their adult plumage within a year and can then start breeding. However, this is certainly not true of all birds.

Sizes and weights

Length: 29cm (11½in).
Weights: cock 88-105g, hen 74-84g.
Ring size: 5.4mm.

53. *Yellow-vented Blue-bonnet; a pure-bred cock. These must not have any chestnut brown on the wings or any red under their tails*

Habitat and habits

Yellow-vented Blue-bonnets are found in open plains, lightly-wooded grassland, dry areas with bushes, and trees along watercourses. They have an irregular distribution, and within their range can be found in some places much more than others. In these places they are rare to fairly common.

They are usually encoutered in pairs or small groups on the ground searching for food, in the shadow of trees or bushes.

When disturbed they raise the feathers on their heads. They are extremely aggressive.

Diet

Insects and larvae provide them with their animal protein; they also eat the seeds of grasses, herb-like plants, and trees, berries and other wild fruit, blossom, and nectar.

Nest-site

In the wild Yellow-venteds nest relatively close to the ground, often at a height of no more than three metres (10ft), and even in fallen trees. In this respect they hardly have to adapt to aviary conditions, as the nest-boxes in them hang at a comparable height. The box should be 50 to 60cm (20 to 24in) high, and have a floor measuring 20cm (8in) square. A 5cm (2in) diameter entrance hole is sufficient.

Breeding process

Both birds take part in choosing a suitable nest site. Once the choice has been made the hen lays four to seven eggs, which she then incubates for about twenty-one days. During this period she is fed regularly by the cock. A few days after the chicks have hatched the cock starts helping to feed them. When the chicks first leave the box after about five weeks, the parents are sometimes very jumpy and agitated.

Blue-bonnets have a habit of breeding activity fairly early; it is not unusual for them to start showing interest in the box in the middle of February, and for eggs to appear shortly afterwards. It is better not to disturb hens once they have started incubating, as they dislike this and are liable to abandon the eggs.

When a cock is in season he may chase aggressively after the hen, and this occasionally has serious consequences. One possible way of helping her is to partly block off the entrance hole to the box with a piece of tree bark. The hen will gnaw this away until she has a hole which is just big enough for her to squeeze through but too small for the cock. By doing this she creates a place of refuge for herself. Many aviculturists always place a piece of bark over the hole whatever the situation, as with Blue-bonnets this increases the urge to breed. Two clutches in one year are rare.

General remarks

Blue-bonnets are probably the most aggressive of all Australian parakeets. They must not be kept in an aviary with other species under any circumstances; they can kill birds even larger than themselves. It is also advisable to place double mesh between the flights to prevent them from squabbling with their neighbours, and causing too great a distraction from breeding. They should not be housed next to related species.

When these birds become excited they raise the feathers on their foreheads and nod their heads.

They are not the easiest birds to breed. Just any random cock and hen in one aviary do not necessarily form a good breeding pair. However, once a pair has been established a great affection grows between them and they often spend a lot of time preening each other.

The Yellow-vented is much less common in avicultural collections than the Red-vented. This might be the reason that there are so many crosses between the two. When purchasing these species of parrot-likes make sure that you are buying pure-bred birds. Pay particular attention to the colour of the wings and the under tail coverts. These must have a solid colour and no patchy patterns.

Mutations

A Yellow Blue-bonnet has been observed in the wild.

RED-VENTED BLUE-BONNET
Psephotus haematogaster haematorrhous

Subspecies
The Red-vented Blue-bonnet is a subspecies of the Yellow-vented. The differences between them are given in the previous description, and are also shown in the photographs of both.

Origin of name
Psephotus: inlaid with mosaic.
Haematogaster: blood-red belly.
Haematorrhous: with flowing blood.
Red-vented: with a red rectum; vent = anus.
Dutch: red-vented blue-bonnet.
German: Rotsteisssittich.

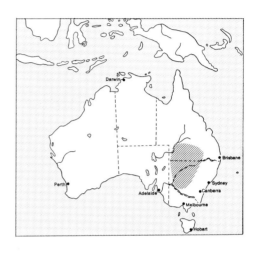

Parents and young
The red on the belly continues down into the under tail coverts; the wing coverts are brownish-red and not olive like those of the Yellow-vented. There is little difference between cocks and hens; cocks may have heavier heads and beaks, and deeper colours. The colouring of young birds is similar to that of their parents, but is sometimes slightly duller, and the reddish-brown on the wings and red on the belly is often rather irregular. The transition to the full adult plumage passes almost unnoticed, although their colours may alter slightly.
Although one-year-old Blue-bonnets are able to reproduce, it mostly takes a year longer.

Sizes and weights
Length: 31cm (12in).
Weights: cock 90-110g, hen 75-90g.
Ring size: 5.4mm.

Habitat and habits
Red-venteds have a greater preference for areas where a reasonable amount of rain falls than either of the other Blue-bonnets. They like open plains with scattered trees and bushes, also tall trees along watercourses.
Just as the Yellow-vents they roam about a great deal in pairs or in small groups, spending a lot of time foraging on the ground. Also during this activity they raise their head feathers when excited.

173

54. Red-vented Blue-bonnet; these are fairly young, not fully-coloured birds. The chestnut brown on the wings will become clearer and the feathers under the tail completely red

Diet

A consequence of their migration to the open plains is that here much of their food is sought. This consists of the seeds of grasses, herb-like plants, bushes and trees, and in addition insects and larvae, blossom, nectar, berries and other wild fruits.

Nest-site

This is very similar to that of the Yellow-vented. An average block measures 50 x 20 x 20cm (20 x 8 x 8in), with a 5cm (2in) entrance hole. If a piece of tree bark is placed partially closing the entrance hole, the hen will chew on it to get in and this will increase the urge to breed.

Breeding process

Four to seven eggs are laid, and incubated by the hen for twenty-one days or thereabouts. They are reasonable sitters, but still rather easily disturbed, so they must have their required peace and quiet. The chicks are fed mainly by the hen, but the cock does help a little when they get older. When they fledge five weeks after hatching they are rather jumpy. It is advisable to remove the fledglings after four weeks to avoid any possible aggression from the cock.

The parents usually call it a day after one clutch; a second is an exception.

General remarks

The same applies here as for the Yellow-vented.

Blue-bonnets are very active birds, they are constantly on the move and spend a lot of time on the ground. A flight four to five metres (13 to 16ft) long meets the requirements of these parrot-likes.

A British aviculturist's experience illustrates how difficult it can be to form a breeding pair: it transpired that his consisted of two hens, despite the fact that they had fed each other and mated. The result was thirteen - naturally unfertilized - eggs.

Yellow- and Red-vented Blue-bonnets are very hardy birds.

Mutations

A still very rare Dilute mutation has been bred in Holland. It looks roughly like a normal bird but is paler. The mode of inheritance is probably sex-linked recessive.

55. Naretha Blue-bonnet; the depth of their colours is the main difference between the cock (left) and the hen (right) of these rare birds

NARETHA BLUE-BONNET
Psephotus haematogaster narethae

Subspecies
The Naretha is a subspecies of the Yellow-vented Blue-bonnet previously described.

Origin of name
Psephotus: inlaid with mosaic.
Haematogaster: blood-red belly.
Narethae: Naretha is a town in southern Australia in the region where this parakeet is found.
Dutch: Naretha blue-bonnet.
German: Narethasittich.

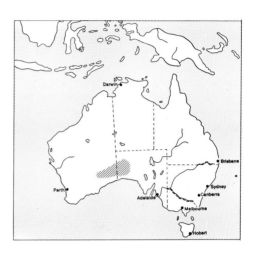

Parents and young
There is no really clearly visible difference between the sexes. The blue on the head and cheeks of the hen is slightly duller and sometimes less extensive, and her head and beak may also be smaller. Unlike the other Blue-bonnets the Naretha does not have a red but a yellow belly. They are noticeably smaller.
Immature birds are a duller version of their parents. The adult plumage starts appearing after about four months. The colours gradually become more beautiful with each moult until they are about four years old. Young cocks and hens can sometimes be told apart by studying the above mentioned differences in head and beak.

Sizes and weights
Length: 28cm (11in).
Weights: cock 75-80g, hen 70g.
Ring size: 5mm.

Habitat and habits
Narethas are found in a rather restricted range in a fairly dry region. They are very reliant on the presence of trees and are rarely found far from them. This region has an annual rainfall of about 200mm (8in), and a relatively temperate climate.

Diet
Although their diet is generally the same as that of the other Blue-bonnets, it seems that it consists for the main part of the seeds of many species of tree.

Nest-site

Cocks and hens look for a suitable nest cavity together, and they always settle for a hollow trunk or branch. In many cases the opening is quite close to the ground, and the nests themselves may even be below ground level. They find a nest-box measuring 45 x 18 x 18cm (18 x 7 x 7in) a suitable alternative. An entrance hole with a diameter of 5cm (2in) is sufficient.

Breeding process

Four to seven eggs are laid and incubated by the hen for about twenty days. Narethas rate as one of the more difficult species and are certainly not birds for the beginner. Hens can be very jumpy during the breeding season, and must be provided with the necessary peace and quiet.

Four weeks after hatching the chicks fledge, and in the wild they then remain with their parents for quite some time.

General remarks

Just as other Blue-bonnets Narethas are aggressive by nature. They must only be kept in pairs and must not have any other aggressive species as neighbours. Even the cock and his mate may sometimes fall out with each other.

GOLDEN-SHOULDERED PARAKEET
Psephotus chrysopterygius chrysopterygius

Subspecies

1. *Psephotus chrysopterygius*
   chrysopterygius
   Golden-shouldered Parakeet
2. *Psephotus chrysopterygius dissimilis*
   Hooded Parakeet

The Hooded Parakeet is described separately. The colour photographs are sufficient to see the difference between the two. A striking characteristic of the Hooded is that its head is completely black; the Golden-shouldered has a yellow band across its forehead. Hens of number 1 are similar in appearance to those of number 2 but have less blue on their cheeks.

Origin of name

Psephotus: inlaid with mosaic.
Chrysopterygius: golden wing.
Dutch: goudschouderparkiet.
German: Goldschultersittich.

Parents and young

The cock is so much more colourful than the hen that there can be no mistaking the sex of adult birds. Cocks lack wing bars, whereas hens have them; however, this is of no importance when determining the sex of these parakeets.

Immature birds present more difficulty. Young birds look very similar to their mother, although males are slightly more brightly-coloured. The bluer cheeks and darker head are particularly noticeable. The juvenile moult at an age of four months often gives more certainty, although young cocks only develop their full plumage when they are fifteen or sixteen months old. Immature birds also have yellowish beaks, which turn to the normal colour after five months.

Cocks which were not yet in full adult plumage have been known to produce offspring, so they may be sexually mature after about a year. However, this is by no means true in all cases.

Sizes and weights

Length: 26cm (10in).
Weights: cock 56g, hen 54g.
Ring size: 5mm.

56. Golden-shouldered Parakeet; a species for the experienced aviculturist

Habitat and habits

Golden-shouldereds live in a very different habitat from most other Australian parakeets. They choose open woodland near extensive plains of sandy ground where termite hills are found. During the rainy season these areas are flooded and, therefore, completely inaccessible. Besides trees, particularly eucalyptuses, there are also bushes and other low-growing plants.

Golden-shouldereds live mainly in pairs or family groups, and are sometimes found in larger flocks where there is an abundance of food or at drinking places. They never wander more than a hundred kilometres from their nest-site.

They are good fliers, but spend a lot of time on the ground searching for grass seeds.

Diet

Golden-shouldereds are specialized in small grass seeds, which they pick up from the ground or remove from the stalks. In addition they eat insects and larvae for the necessary animal protein.

Nest-site

In Australia Golden-shouldered Parakeets nest in the termite hills which are found in many places on the dark, flat surface of their distribution range. They dig a tunnel about 50 cm (20 ins) long and at the end a larger nest cavity. All this activity takes place in the rainy season, as only then are the termite hills soft enough for the holes to be excavated. The rest of the year they are like stone. As the area is partly flooded during the rainy season, the clutch is protected against its predators, and an abundance of seeding grass is available for the parents and young.

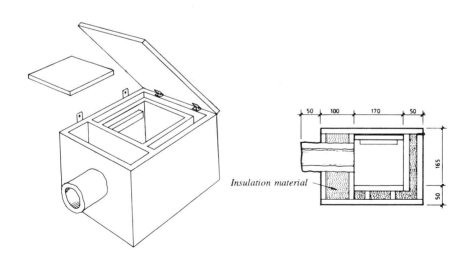

Insulation material

A nest-box for the Golden-shouldered and the Hooded Parakeets. It is as it were a box within a box with insulation in between. It can be made of, for example, 15mm multiplex
(drawn by John Buchan in 'Australian Aviculture', October 1986; reprinted with the kind permission of 'The Avicultural Society of Australia')

57. *Golden-shouldered Parakeet; an immature cock and hen which are beginning to develop their colouring*

The nest is dug about one and a half metres (5ft) above ground and the tunnel to the nest cavity has a diameter of 4 to 5cm (1.5 to 2in).

A copy of this construction must be made for the aviary. This means that the box must measure about 25 x 15 x 15cm (10 x 6 x 6in), and that a pipe must be fitted in the entrance hole to form the tunnel to the nest. The inside diameter need not be bigger than 5cm (2in). The hen requires very little nest material in the box.

Breeding process

In our climate rearing young Golden-shouldereds is no easy matter. As it is very warm inside the termite hills in their distribution range in Australia, hens leave the nest for long periods soon after the eggs have hatched. They have retained this habit in captivity, and this means that in aviaries there is a chance the chicks will undercool and die. Some hens leave the nest as soon as the eggs hatch, others after two weeks. The experiences of aviculturists in western Europe have led to the conclusion that Golden-shouldereds can only be successfully bred if heating is used. The best way of providing the required temperature is to install a thermostatically controlled heating element in the nest-box in such a way that the birds cannot get to it. In the wild the temperature in the nest cavity is more than 30°C. An aviculturist with a lot of experience with these birds achieved the best results with the following schedule: three days before the eggs are due to hatch turn the heating on and set it at 25°, two days before hatching at 29°, and one day before hatching at 33°; keep it at 33° for the first three weeks, then at 31° for the third week, 29° for the fourth, 26° for the fifth; then three days at 23°, two days at 21°, and then at 18° until the chicks fledge. After they have left the box the temperature can be reduced to 13° and if the outside temperature drops under 8° at night, the chicks should be returned to the box at dusk.

Other possible solutions are to set the block on a hot plate, or to fit an infra-red lamp onto the box.

Three to six eggs hatch in about twenty-one days. Both parents feed the chicks in the nest. The chicks fledge in about five weeks, and in the wild they remain with their parents for quite some time and travel about as a family group. In aviaries this is not always possible, as the cock may become rather aggressive. It is advisable to separate parents and young after three to four weeks.

In the wild Golden-shouldered Parakeets sometimes nest very close to each other. One case is reported in which three nests were found within a radius of 50cm. It is a good idea to take this habit into account in the aviary, as it seems that the breeding activities of one pair can be highly contagious. This means that you have much more chance of success if you keep more than one pair. The best situation seems to be to house the pairs next to each other , but to have a solid partition between, so that the birds can hear but not see their neighbours.

Observations in the wild have shown that chicks are not fed with dry seeds, but always with unripe seeds. Birds in aviaries must be provided with soaked and sprouting seeds.

General remarks

Golden-shouldered Parakeets are suitable only for the experienced birdkeeper. As these birds originate from a tropical area they are not keen on cold and damp.

According to the Washington Convention the Golden-shouldered is a threatened species. There has been a reduction in their numbers since the beginning of the century.

These parrot-likes benefit by a layer of coarse sand on the floor of their aviary from 5 to 10cm (2 to 4in) deep.

HOODED PARAKEET
Psephotus chrysopterygius dissimilis

Subspecies
The Hooded Parakeet is a subspecies of the previously described Golden-shouldered Parakeet. Cock Golden-shouldereds have a yellow band on their foreheads, but the Hoodeds do not. Hen Hoodeds have a greyish-green crown, whereas the Golden-shoulders' is brownish; hen Golden-shouldereds have less blue on their cheeks.

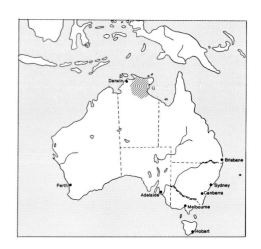

Origin of name
Psephotus: inlaid with mosaic.
Chrysopterygius: golden wing.
Dissimilis: not the same.
Dutch: hooded parkiet.
German: Hoodedsittich.

Parents and young
In his adult plumage the cock is much more colourful than the hen. Young birds look very similar to their mother. Young males can sometimes be picked out by their slightly bluer cheeks; however, this is not true in all cases, and breeders and buyers are sometimes confronted with unpleasant surprises. After about four months the juvenile moult takes place, and this sometimes produces greater differences in colour. As young males grow older they give their sex away by their behaviour: they soon start acting rather excitedly, they squabble more, draw themselves up, and shake their tails now and then. They develop their full adult plumage in twelve to sixteen months.
Hoodeds are usually sexually mature at two years of age, but it is not unheard of for offspring to be brought into the world after a year.

Sizes and weights
Length: 26cm (10in).
Weights: cock 50-60g, hen 54-59g.
Ring size: 5mm.

Habitat and habits
Their distribution range is in northern Australia, in areas where termite hills are found in open woodland and extensive grassland. Hoodeds can be seen here in pairs or family groups, and sometimes in larger numbers where food is abundant and at drinking places.

With the approach of the breeding season the birds separate into breeding pairs.
These parakeets spend a lot of time in trees, but find most of their food on the ground.
Just like the Golden-shouldereds they probably never go more than a hundred kilometres
from their nest sites. Their numbers are decreasing.
Both cocks and hens are able to raise their crown feathers into a small crest, and do so
during the excitement of courtship.

Diet
Hooded Parakeets are specialized in small grass seeds which they pick up from the ground
or take from the stalks. They also eat insects and greenery.
They have carried their preference for small seeds into the aviary and, apart from green
food, it is difficult to get them on to anything else. They must be provided with soaked
and sprouted seeds, particularly if they have chicks.

Nest-site
These parrot-likes have the same breeding habits as the Golden-shouldereds; the nest is at
the end of a tunnel dug out in a termite hill. Please refer to the Golden-shouldered
Parakeet for a more detailed description.

*58. Hooded Parakeet; in the wild they nest in termite hills, the same as Golden-shouldereds. In Europe they
prefer to breed in autumn*

The same applies to the nest-box; make sure that the size is not bigger than that given, as smaller boxes retain the warmth better, and because in the wild the space is also very limited.

Breeding process

Hooded Parakeets have not adjusted to our climate by breeding in the spring. Most of them only get the urge to breed in September, which means that by the time the chicks hatch it is getting colder. This can lead to the same problems as with the Golden-shouldereds, and all the more as the hen leaves the chicks alone in the nest for long periods shortly after the eggs have hatched. The risks become greater the later it is in the year, and breeding may go into early spring. Some form of heating is, therefore, essential. Generally speaking the hen spends the greater part of the first week in the box. After that, however, the chicks are not able to keep themselves and each other warm. Luckily more and more birds are appearing which start their breeding activity in the spring. Once the three to six eggs have been laid they take about three weeks to hatch. The cock feeds the hen both outside the box and on the nest.

Thirty days after hatching the chicks are fledged and they leave the box. In the wild they then form family groups which remain together for some time. In aviaries this is less successful as the cock soon starts chasing his sons about. Therefore, it is better to remove the young birds from the aviary about three or four weeks after they have left the box.

As with Golden-shouldereds, keeping more than one pair of Hoodeds has a favourable effect as they stimulate each other in their breeding activities.

General remarks

Hooded Parakeets are for the more experienced birdkeeper. At one time they were rather fragile, but nowadays it is no longer a problem, and in that respect now compare favourably with, for example, the Red-rumped or Many-coloured Parakeets.

They can be very aggressive, particularly in the breeding season, and are not afraid of larger birds.

The flight must be at least four metres (13ft) long in order to show these exceptionally beautiful parakeets to their best advantage.

It is not advisable to form a pair with two birds of which one was born in spring and the other in autumn, as the timing of their reproductive cycles will not coincide.

Genus *Cyanoramphus*

The members of this genus, the Kakarikis, are found in New Caledonia, New Zealand and on its many surrounding islands, Norfolk Island, and a number of subantarctic islands; but not on the Australian continent.

They are all very active birds which are constantly on the move; they walk along their perches at high speed, and climb up and down the wire mesh without using their beaks. They have very long legs; this is an indication to the fact that they spend a lot of time on the ground, where they scratch the earth like chickens. They are very fond of eating greenery, and are enthusiastic bathers.

Cocks and hens have the same colouring. Cocks are best distinguished by their heavier heads and beaks, and they are slightly larger.

This genus comprises six species, two of which are extinct. Two subspecies have also died out. This concerns numbers 6, 8, 13 and 14.

Numbers 2 and 10 are the only two species to be found in avicultural collections. The others are not kept here and are, therefore, not further dealt with.

genus	species	subspecies	
Cyanoramphus	*unicolor*	-	1. Antipodes Green Kakariki
"	*novaezelandiae*	*novaezelandiae*	2. Red-fronted Kakariki
"	"	*cyanurus*	3. Kermadec Red-fronted Kakariki
"	"	*chathamensis*	4. Chatham Red-fronted Kakariki
"	"	*hochstetteri*	5. Antipodes Red-fronted Kakariki
"	"	*erythrotis*	6. Macquarie Red-fronted Kakariki
"			
"	"	*cookii*	7. Norfolk Red-fronted Kakariki
"	"	*subflavescens*	8. Lord Howe Red-fronted Kakariki
"	"	*saisetti*	9. New Caledonia Red-fronted Kakariki
"	*auriceps*	*auriceps*	10. Yellow-fronted Kakariki
"	"	*forbesi*	11. Chatham Yellow-fronted Kakariki
"	*malherbi*	-	12. Orange-fronted Kakariki
"	*zealandicus*	-	13. Black-fronted Kakariki
"	*ulietanus*	-	14. Society Kakariki

59. *Red-fronted Kakariki; the cock is larger. He is shown here together with a Cinnamon hen*

RED-FRONTED KAKARIKI

Cyanoramphus novaezelandiae

Subspecies
1. *Cyanoramphus novaezelandiae*
   novaezelandiae
   Red-fronted Kakariki
2. *Cyanoramphus novaezelandiae*
   cyanurus
   Kermadec Red-fronted Kakariki
3. *Cyanoramphus novaezelandiae*
   chathamensis
   Chatham Red-fronted Kakariki
4. *Cyanoramphus novaezelandiae*
   hochstetteri
   Antipodes Red-fronted Kakariki
5. *Cyanoramphus novaezelandiae*
   erythrotis
   Macquarie Red-fronted Kakariki
6. *Cyanoramphus novaezelandiae cookii*   - Norfolk Red-fronted Kakariki
7. *Cyanoramphus novaezelandiae subflavescens*   - Lord Howe Red-fronted Kakariki
8. *Cyanoramphus novaezelandiae saisetti*   - New Caledonia Red-fronted Kakariki

There is little point in mentioning the - slight - differences between all the subspecies here. Only number 1, the nominative form, is found in collections, and will, therefore, be described. Numbers 5 and 7 are extinct.

Origin of name
Cyanoramphus: blue beak.
Novaezelandiae: New Zealand.
Kakariki: small parakeet, the name that the Maoris gave to this bird.
Dutch: roodvoorhoofdkakariki.
German: Ziegenzittich.

Parents and young
Cocks and hens have the same colouring, but the cocks are slightly larger and have more powerful heads and beaks. Hens sometimes have a little less red behind their eyes. Adult males do not have wing bars, whereas most females do. Young birds look very similar to their parents. They have a little less red on their heads and shorter tails; moreover, the colour of their beaks is slightly lighter. Generally speaking Kakarikis are sexually mature by one year old. However, they have been bred in captivity for so long that this period is getting shorter and shorter. There are even hens which breed at four months, and three-month-old cocks which fertilize the eggs. However, to allow this to happen is not good for the birds' development. It is much more preferable to make them wait until the following season by not making a nest-box available to them before then.

189

Sizes and weights
Length: 28cm (11in).
Weights: 60g.
Ring size: 5.4mm.

Habitat and habits
Red-fronted Kakarikis have become rare in New Zealand and are now only found in the larger areas of forest. They spend most of the day searching for food in the tops of trees and the outside branches of bushes. They often alight on the ground to pick up seeds. They are tame and can be approached closely.

Diet
Kakarikis principally eat the seeds and fruits of a variety of trees and bushes, but they also tuck into blossom, leaves, and blades of grass.
Studies have shown that their menu in the wild has a high protein content. In an aviary they must be given large amounts of green food.

Nest-site
In the wild most Kakarikis nest in hollow trees; however, on the islands round New Zealand they often make use of cracks in the rocks.
In an aviary a nest-box measuring 35 x 18 x 18cm (14 x 7 x 7in) and with an entrance hole of no more than 6cm (2.5in) is sufficient. These parakeets are not in the least choosy.

Breeding process
The Kakariki is a very fertile bird, and a clutch numbers between five and nine eggs. They make exemplary parents, and the chicks which hatch out of these eggs are excellently reared. Incubation takes nineteen or twenty days and is done by the hen alone. During this period the cock feeds her through the entrance hole or outside the box. Once the chicks have hatched he enters the box more often. The chicks fledge about thirty-five days after hatching. Kakarikis are able to rear a number of clutches in one season.

General remarks
These parakeets adapt to aviaries very well, and can be kept by any birdkeeper. They are exceptionally suitable for beginners. They are not aggressive and can even be kept in mixed company, though the best results are still achieved if they are housed separately in pairs, as they can become so distracted that they rather forget their duties, and sometimes disturb other inhabitants in their breeding activity. They forage on the ground a great deal and scratch about in a chicken-like fashion; as a result they are rather prone to worm infestations. They sometimes scratch about in their seed containers, so throwing out all the contents. These must, therefore, be shaped in such a way that this is not possible. They must also have a lot of bathing water. Kakarikis are very inquisitive and as a result they become very tame, especially if time is spent on this aspect. I have had young birds that even hung on the buttons of my coat when I was in the aviary.

They have a characteristic call, which is very easily recognised, and rather resembles the bleating of a goat. The German name is derived from this: Ziegensittich = Goat Parakeet.

Unfortunately in the past too many Red-fronted and Yellow-fronted Kakarikis were crossed and then sold as pure-bred birds. These crosses are distinguishable by the red and yellow on their heads; the red is either orangeish or the two colours run over into each other. Avoid such birds; if you buy them you will be going about your hobby the wrong way. There are enough pure-bred birds available.

Another point is the size of the Kakariki. The overbreeding of these birds has resulted in a considerable reduction in size; this is also partly due to too much inbreeding. If you wish to breed these parakeets, look for large unrelated birds.

It is also worth mentioning that Kakarikis make excellent foster parents. However, make sure that any eggs trusted to their care are not from a much bigger species.

Finally, do not be surprised if your Kakarikis miss a breeding season, as they for some unexplained reason sometimes do. This is of course nothing to panic about: the following year they begin again from where they left off.

Mutations

A Pied Red-fronted Kakariki has been around for some time. There is also a Cinnamon mutation, as shown in the photograph. This bird inherits sex-linked recessive. The chicks have red eyes on hatching which begin to turn darker after about three days. There is also a Yellow mutation.

60. Yellow-fronted Kakariki; this cock is slightly larger than the hen. An easy species for the beginner

YELLOW-FRONTED KAKARIKI

Cyanoramphus auriceps

Subspecies

1. *Cyanoramphus auriceps auriceps*
        Yellow-fronted Kakariki
2. *Cyanoramphus auriceps forbesi*
        Chatham Yellow-fronted Kakariki
Only number 1 is found in collections here. Number 2 is slightly larger, has a more brightly-coloured plumage with more yellow on the belly feathers, and the stripe on the forehead does not reach the eyes.

Origin of name

Cyanoramphus: blue beak.
Auriceps: golden head.
Forbesi: after Dr Henry Ogg Forbes (1853 - 1932), who, as a botanist and ethnologist, made expeditions to Indonesia and New Guinea.
Kakariki: small parakeet, the name which the Maoris gave to this bird.
Dutch: geelvoorhoofdkakariki.
German: Springsittich.

Parents and young

Unlike the Red-fronted Kakariki, the Yellow-fronted does not have any red behind the eye. It does possess a red stripe across its forehead with a yellow patch above it. The name Yellow-fronted Kakariki is therefore not strictly correct.
Cocks and hens are virtually alike. Males are slightly larger, their stripe is brighter red and they have a little more yellow. The iris of the cock is sometimes deeper red than that of the hen. Head and beak are also slightly heavier.
Immature Kakarikis are slightly smaller and the red and yellow is duller. After six months the cocks have more yellow on their heads.
The same applies for sexual maturity as for the Red-fronted Kakariki; do not allow them to breed until the season after they have hatched.

Sizes and weights

Length: 25cm (10in).
Weights: 55g.
Ring size: 5.4mm.

Habitat and habits

Yellow-fronted Kakarikis are fairly common in the larger areas of mountain forests. It is not surprising that they have a lot in common with the Red-fronted; however, they are more dependent on trees for their food and less on low-growing plants.

Diet

Yellow-fronted Kakarikis are not particular with regard to their diet.
The menu consists mainly of seeds, berries and other fruits, blossom, green food, also some insects and larvac.

Nest-site

Little is known about the situation in the wild, but it is probably similar to that of the Red-fronted Kakariki. In an aviary they can be supplied with a box measuring 35 x 18 x 18cm (14 x 7 x 7in); the diameter of the entrance hole does not need to be more than 6cm (2.5in).

Breeding process

The number of eggs varies from five to nine, although there are of course exceptions. The hen incubates them for nineteen or twenty days and then conscientiously rears the chicks with the cock. Together they see to it that the young birds are able to leave the box within five weeks; by this time the eggs for the next clutch may have already been laid. Three clutches in one year should be considered the maximum; if the birds go on after this the keeper should take action.

General remarks

In many respects Yellow-fronted Kakarikis can be compared to their direct relatives, the Red-fronted Kakarikis. The greater part which is mentioned about them also applies here. The keeper of Yellow-fronts is, therefore, advised to read that section of this book as well.
Yellow-fronted Kakarikis are less popular than Red-fronted. This is possibly due to their smaller size; most aviculturists like to have the more heavily-built birds. However, it is often difficult to fathom why one species is more in demand than another.
The number of the subspecies of this bird, number 2, in the wild has dropped to about fifty, and it is therefore listed as endangered under the Washington Convention.
Kakarikis are hardy aviary birds. As they are so active they do not need too large an aviary. A length of two and a half to three metres (8 to 10ft) is sufficient.

Genus *Eunymphicus*

The Horned Parakeets of this genus are only found on a few islands in the Pacific, northeast of Australia. They are very rarely found in collections and, what is more, they are listed as endangered according to the Washington Convention.

They are principally green with black and/or red on their heads. The couple of extra long feathers on the crown which form a sort of tuft is characteristic of the genus. This cannot be raised.

Horned Parakeets are similar to Kakarikis in their habits. There is no difference in colouring between cocks and hens.

genus	species	subspecies	
Eunymphicus	*cornutus*	*cornutus*	1. Horned Parakeet
"	"	*uvaeensis*	2. Ouvea Horned Parakeet

61. Horned Parakeet; the colouring is the same, but the cock (right) is slightly larger

HORNED PARAKEET - *Eunymphicus cornutus*

Subspecies

1. *Eunymphicus cornutus cornutus*
                 Horned Parakeet
2. *Eunymphicus cornutus uvaeensis*
                 Ouvea Horned Parakeet

Number 1 is shown in the photograph. It has more red on its head and the tuft consists of two black feathers with red tips. It is found in New Caledonia. Number 2 has much less red and more black on its head; the tuft consists of six green feathers. This subspecies is found on the island of Ouvea.

Origin of name

Eunymphicus: like a lovely nymph.
Cornutus: horned.
Uvaeensis: from the island of Ouvea.
Dutch: hoornparkiet.
German: Hornsittich.

Parents and young

The sexes are none too easy to tell apart. A skilful observer is usually able to see that the cock's head and beak are a touch heavier and the crown feathers slightly longer. The colouring of immature birds is virtually the same as that of the parents, only a little duller. However, they are easily distinguishable by their yellowish beaks, dark eyes, and shorter tufts. Their beaks turn black when they are about nine months old. Although as a rule Horned Parakeets are sexually mature after two years, one-year-old birds do sometimes rear young. It seems that young hens are more likely to do this than cocks.

Sizes and weights

Length: 33cm (13in).
Weights: 80g.
Ring size: 5.4mm.

Habitat and habits

Little is known about the lifestyle of this species in the wild. They live in damp woodlands; the area of which is unfortunately decreasing. Their habits are difficult to observe as they live in pairs or in small family groups, and their green colouring makes them difficult to spot. They do come down to the ground in search of food.

Horned Parakeets are fairly closely related to Kakarikis, and their habits are, therefore, very similar.

Diet
In the wild their diet consists of fruit, blossom, nectar, unripe seeds, and various parts of plants. The aviculturist must take this into account, and on top of their seed mix they should be provided with relatively large amounts of berries and other fruits.

Nest-site
In the wild they nest in hollow branches or trunks. In the aviary a nest box 50 to 80cm (20 to 30in) tall and 25cm (10in) square can be used. Breeding success has also been achieved with a box 100cm (40in) tall. A 7cm (3in) diameter entrance hole is sufficient.

Breeding process
A clutch numbers two to four eggs. These are incubated by the hen for about twenty days; during this period she is regularly fed by the cock. The fledglings leave the box about forty days after hatching; a week later they begin to feed, and in another two or three weeks they can fend for themselves. However, they go on begging their parents for food for some time afterwards. As they form family groups in the wild, it is a good idea to let the parents and young stay together for some time; this is good for the development of social behaviour, and there is no danger of birds of this species becoming aggressive towards each other.
In western Europe Horned Parakeets start breeding quite late; often as late as the end of May.

General remarks
The Horned Parakeet is protected by the Washington Convention
and, therefore, may not be kept without a licence. The existence of particularly the subspecies *Eunymphicus cornutus uvaeensis* is threatened, and it is much rarer than the nominative form in Europe.
Horned Parakeets are peaceful and fairly active birds. They are very tolerant, also to birds of their own species. Nevertheless, it is better not to house two pairs in adjoining aviaries, as then they might distract each other. They are very adventurous and examine every nook and cranny of their accommodation. So in this respect too, they have a lot in common with the Kakarikis.
Once they are properly acclimatized, and with a closable night shelter, these birds can come through a normal winter without supplementary heating.

Genus *Neophema*

Three clear groups can be distinguished within this well-known genus:
1. the Bourke's Parakeet. This occupies a somewhat anomalous position within the genus, and is a completely different colour than the rest. No general agreement exists as to whether it belongs to the Neophemas. Some experts consider it to be a seperate genus, *Neopsephotus*;
2. four species with a characteristic blue stripe across the forehead, which are otherwise very similar: the Blue-winged, the Elegant, the Orange-bellied and the Rock Grass Parakeet. The last two are not to be found in collections; the Orange-bellied is listed in the Washington Convention as endangered;
3. two species with extensive blue on the head and reddish brown on wings and/or breast. There is a clear difference between cocks and hens. These are the Turquoisine and Splendid Grass Parakeets.

All seven species are ground feeders which live in fairly open country in the wild and avoid woodland. The sexual dimorphism (difference between cock and hen) ranges from great to slight. There are no subspecies within this genus.

Five of the seven species are widely known and kept. It is possible to house them mixed with birds of other genuses. More than one pair of Neophemas together is not advisable, as this can lead to aggression and crosses.

genus	species	subspecies	
Neophema	*bourkii*	-	1. Bourke's Parakeet
"	*chrysostoma*	-	2. Blue-winged Grass Parakeet
"	*elegans*	-	3. Elegant Grass Parakeet
"	*petrophila*	-	4. Rock Grass Parakeet
"	*chrysogaster*	-	5. Orange-bellied Grass Parakeet
"	*pulchella*	-	6. Turquoisine Grass Parakeet
"	*splendida*	-	7. Splendid Grass Parakeet

62. *Bourke's Parakeet; an exceptionally fine Rosa pair*

BOURKE'S PARAKEET - *Neophema bourkii*

Subspecies
None.

Origin of name
Neophema: new sound.
Bourkii: this bird is named after Fort Bourke, from where Thomas Livingstone Mitchell (1792-1855) undertook the expeditions during which he discovered the species in 1838. Sir Richard Bourke (1777-1855) was Governor of the Australian state of New South Wales.
Dutch: Bourkeparkiet.
German: Bourkesittich.

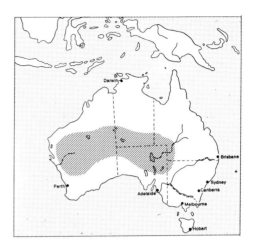

Parents and young
At first sight the cock and hen look very similar, but a more careful inspection reveals some slight differences. The hen generally has a wing bar, the cock either has none or a very light one. The cock has got a blue stripe above its beak, though its clarity varies. The colour of the belly of the hen is duller. The colouring is rather variable. When their wings are spread it becomes apparent that the flight feathers of the cock show much more blue than those of the hens.
Immature birds look like the hen, though they have less pink on their bellies. It is very difficult to determine the sex; hens usually have a clearer wing bar. Blue feathers start to appear on the heads of cocks after the first moult at about five months. They gain their full plumage after eight or nine months, and are able to produce young the following breeding season.

Sizes and weights
Length: 21cm (8.5in).
Weights: cock 47-49g, hen 42-49g.
Ring size: 4mm.

Habitat and habits
The Bourke's Parakeet prefers arid and semi-arid areas containing acacia bushes where the annual rainfall does not exceed 250mm (10in). It is a typical example of the wildlife found in the Australian interior. Under ideal feeding conditions (after sufficient rain) the density of Bourke's Parakeets can become great over a wide range. As the food situation worsens their numbers can reduce dramatically. These birds are not often observed in the wild, as they are at home in an area that is not inhabited and which few people visit; a second

reason is that they are most active in the early morning and at dusk, and are inconspicuous, partly due to their good camouflage. They are even active at night, particularly if the moon is clear. The observer can then even hear them flying. Their nocturnal habits explain why these parakeets have such large eyes.

They are usually found in pairs or small groups, but in times of drought a hundred or more can be seen at watering places. They roam about, and as their movements depend on the weather conditions, it is virtually impossible to predict where they are to be found.

In captivity they have retained the behaviour described here; during the day they are very quiet, and they become active towards dusk and at dawn.

Diet

These birds get the majority of their food from the ground. They have a preference for the seeds of a variety of grasses, but also feed on herb-like plants, bushes, and to a lesser extent trees. They undoubtably gobble up the odd insect.

Nest-site

In the wild they generally search for cavities in trees at a height of one to three metres, although entrance holes have been found only 30cm above ground level. They seldom go higher than three metres. In an aviary they have no objection to a 30cm (12in) tall box with a floor area measuring 15 x 15cm (6 x 6in); a 5cm (2in) entrance hole is sufficient.

Breeding process

Bourke's Parakeets are easy to breed; they can be bred in colonies, but housing pairs seperately is better. Once they have chosen a suitable box three to six eggs are laid. The incubation time is about eighteen days, and during that period the hen hardly leaves the nest. She comes out only once a day in order to eat or be fed by the cock, and to defecate. The chicks leave the nest a good four weeks after hatching, and in the wild they remain with their parents for some time. In an aviary often a second, and sometimes even a third, clutch follows, and then it is better to place the now independent young alone.

Bourke's Parakeets are relatively messy nesters. If the situation gets too bad, the nesting material should be replaced.

General remarks

As I mentioned earlier some people regard the Bourke's Parakeet as a seperate genus. One of the reasons is that it has never been satisfactorily proved that it can be crossbred with other Neophemas. Another point is that their behaviour and colour differ.

As an argument against this theory, it can be said that this parakeet shows many similarities to other *Neophema* species: it has the same posture and size; and the size of the clutch, and the incubation and fledging times do not differ. This theory holds as the colour difference is due to an adjustment to the habitat, and is, therefore, of lesser importance.

What is more important to the average birdkeeper than this discussion is that it is an ideal bird for everbody, and particularly for beginners. They are hardy, and can be regarded as reliable breeders. Bourke's Parakeets can also be of great use as foster parents to other Neophemas and smaller parakeets.

They are not aggressive but rather tolerant and loving, and can be housed in an aviary three metres (10ft) long. If you wish to reconstruct their natural habitat, bushes and dry twigs can be placed in the flight, and they will spend many hours a day secluded in them. A sandy floor with grass and other short herbs and plants completes the scene.

As birds of the desert this species used to be susceptible to our damp cold, but as a result of years of breeding this vulnerability has disappeared. What is a problem is that the quality of these birds has declined; many are too small and have too little colour. A great deal of attention must, therefore, be paid to these points, and in that respect it is often best to purchase at exhibitions.

Mutations

At the moment there are four mutations available to the aviculturist: Yellow, Isabel, Fallow and Rosa.

The Yellow Bourke has a light yellow back and wings; head and breast are a faded pink. The claws are so light they appear translucent. Cocks are darker than hens, with the latter giving a more yellow impression. The mode of inheritance is autosomal recessive.

The Isabel mutation looks similar to the Yellow, but has more pink and less yellow, which also tends to a brownish-yellow. Legs and claws are greyish. The eyes are red, as are those of the Yellow mutation. The mode of inheritance is sex-linked recessive.

The Fallow also belongs to the yellow series. It looks a lot like the Isabel, but the colouring is sometimes duller. It also has red eyes. The Fallow has an off-white beak, the isabel's is yellower. It inherits autosomal recessive.

The Rosa Bourke is in fact an Opaline mutation. The amount of pink displayed can vary quite considerably. It inherits sex-linked recessive.

63. Bourke's Parakeet; Yellow mutation

64. Bourke's Parakeet; Normal cock with a good blue stripe above its beak

65. *Blue-winged Grass Parakeet; the colouring of the cock (left) is deeper*

BLUE-WINGED GRASS PARAKEET
Neophema chrysostoma

Subspecies
None.

Origin of name
Neophema: new noise.
Chrysostoma: golden beak.
Dutch: blauwvleugelparkiet.
German: Feinsittich.

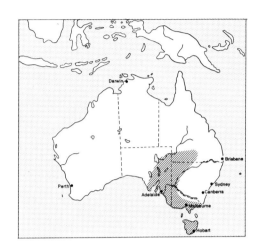

Parents and young
The cock has a deep blue stripe across its forehead which reaches as far as the eyes; the hen's is smaller. The lores, the area between the beak and the eyes, are yellow and a small patch of yellow is also visible behind the eyes. The underside of the wings of the cocks is darker than that of the hens. The general plumage of the cock is deeper and it has more blue on the wings. Usually neither of them has a wing bar.
Immature birds are a duller version of the hen. Neither sex has much blue on its forehead, so it is difficult to tell the sexes apart. They develop their full adult plumage after eight or nine months. They are sexually mature after one year.

Sizes and weights
Length: 21cm (8.5in).
Weights: cock 48-61g, hen 44-49g.
Ring size: 4mm.

Habitat and habits
The Blue-winged is the least specialized of the Neophemas, and can be found in a variety of habitats; ranging from the green mountains of Tasmania to the arid interior of Australia, and in between savannahs, lightly-wooded hills, valleys, grassland with scattered trees, and coastal areas. They are common. The population can probably be divided into two groups; one breeds in southeast Australia and the other migrates to Tasmania.
Blue-wings live in pairs or small groups; in the winter they sometimes move around in larger flocks. They spend the majority of their time on the ground foraging for food.

Diet
These parakeets live on the seeds of grasses and herb-like plants, blossom, berries and other fruits, insects and larvae.

Nest-site

In the wild a number of nests is sometimes found in the hollow branches and trunk of one tree. They will readily accept a nest box measuring 30 x 15 x 15cm (12 x 6 x 6in) and with a 5cm (2in) entrance hole.

Breeding process

If a number of pairs is kept they tend to stimulate each other into breeding activity with their calls and behaviour. Particularly pairs which are housed together in one aviary show more activity than a single pair.

The four to six eggs are incubated for eighteen to nineteen days by the hen. They sit very tight and are regularly fed by the cock, in the box as well as outside it. When the chicks have hatched and are a few days old the cock also helps in the feeding. After the fledglings leave the box about four weeks after hatching they remain with the parents for some time. A second clutch often follows.

General remarks

At first sight Blue-wings and Elegants look very much alike. However, there are several differences which guarantee correct identification. The plumage of the Blue-wing is slightly duller and has less yellow on the belly; the blue on the wings is more extensive and deeper. The most reliable indications are found on the head. The blue stripe across the forehead reaches as far as the eyes, and a yellow patch is visible behind the eyes. The blue stripe across the Elegant's forehead runs through and past the eyes. The photographs show these differences clearly.

When Blue-wings are in breeding condition their plumage appears brighter. This is because they moult shortly before the breeding season.

As these parakeets are not very active, it is better not to provide them with too many seeds with a high oil content, otherwise they become overweight.

A flight three metres (10ft) long is sufficient. In a bigger flight they can be housed with other non-aggressive birds. They are hardy birds, and our climate presents no problems.

66. Blue-winged Grass Parakeet; this species has no blue behind or above the eyes, but does have yellow. Compare photo 67

67. Elegant Grass Parakeet; this bird has no yellow behind or above the eyes, but does have blue. Compare photo 66

68. *Elegant Grass Parakeet; the cock (left) is generally slightly yellower*

ELEGANT GRASS PARAKEET - *Neophema elegans*

Subspecies
None.

Origin of name
Neophema: new noise.
Elegans: elegant.
Dutch: elegantparkiet.
German: Schmucksittich.

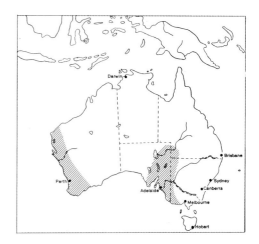

Parents and young
The stripe across the forehead of the cock is deep blue, and above it is a paler blue stripe which reaches to behind the eyes. The hen also has this but it is less clear.
Usually neither sex has a wing bar; if one is visible you will be looking at a hen.
The colours of the cock are deeper, and there is a chance that he will have an orangeish patch on his belly.
Young birds are duller and the forehead stripe is only just visible. They develop their full plumage in a little over six months. The plumage will become more beautiful every year for about seven years. Once they have reached adulthood cocks can be seen to have dark flight feathers, whereas those of the hens have a light edging.
Elegants reach sexual maturity in one year.

Sizes and weights
Length: 22cm (8.5in).
Weights: cock 42-51g, hen 42-44g.
Ring size: 4mm.

Habitat and habits
Elegants prefer open or semi-open areas; grassland with scattered trees, areas with acacia and eucalyptus bushes, salt-loving vegetation, and sandy coastal areas. They search on the ground for food and are superbly camouflaged for this activity. They are fairly shy and difficult to approach.
Outside the breeding season they sometimes form large flocks of up to a hundred birds, sometimes in the company of Blue-wings where their distribution ranges overlap. With the approach of the breeding season they divide up into pairs or small groups.

Diet
They find most of their food on the ground: this consists of seeds of grasses and herb-like plants, greenery, berries and other small wild fruits, also all manner of insects.

69. Elegant Grass Parakeet; Lutino mutation

Nest-site

In the wild they nest in hollow branches and trunks, usually not far above ground.
If you supply a box measuring 30 x 15 x 15cm (12 x 6 x 6in) with a 5cm (2.5in) diameter entrance hole, they should rear their young in it.

Breeding process

The nesting behaviour is on the whole the same as that of the Blue-wings. Four or five eggs are laid in the box, which should not contain too much nesting material. The incubation time is about eighteen days, after which period the chicks see the light of day for the first time. The hen sits very tight and is fed both on the nest and outside the box by the cock. He also assists with the feeding of the chicks once they are a few days old, and they leave the box after a good four weeks. In many cases a second clutch then follows.

General remarks

The differences between the Elegant and the Blue-winged have already been mentioned, and therefore do not need to be dealt with here.
Elegant Grass Parakeets are reliable breeding and aviary birds, which are admirably suitable for the inexperienced birdkeeper to start with. Our climate does not cause any problems, but they must have a closable night shelter available.
It is better not to house them with other Neophemas as there is a chance of crosses occurring. They can be kept in larger aviaries together with other non-aggressive species. When housed in pairs a flight three metres (10ft) long is spacious enough.

Mutations

Unlike the Blue-winged there is already a number of Elegant mutations, among others the Yellow-Pied, Dilute-Green, Cinnamon, and Lutino.
The Yellow-Pied has a dominant mode of inheritance, this means that Pied chicks may result from breeding with a normal bird. There is no question of these being split birds. The Pied is still very little known.
The Dilute-Green and the Cinnamon are also still very rare; they inherit autosomal recessive and sex-linked recessive respectively.
The Lutino has been known for longer; it is pure yellow with red eyes, and has white feathers where those of the normal bird are blue. Unlike most lutinos this form of the Elegant does not inherit sex-linked but autosomal recessive. This means that both sexes can be split for lutino.

70. Turquoisine Grass Parakeet; the cock is easiest to identify by his reddish-brown wing bar

TURQUOISINE GRASS PARAKEET - *Neophema pulchella*

Subspecies
None.

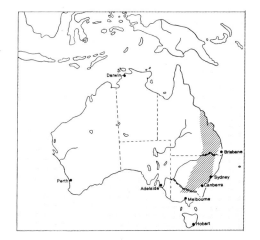

Origin of name
Neophema: new sound.
Pulchella: pretty, fine.
Dutch: turquoisineparkiet.
German: Schönsittich.

Parents and young
Although the parents resemble each other, there are nevertheless several striking differences; the cock is deeper in colour and has a reddish-brown bar on its wings. It does not have a stripe on its underwing, whereas the hen often does.
These differences are often visible on young birds. It is true that they look a lot like the hen, but males have a faint wing bar and a slightly bluer head.
They develop their full plumage within six months, and they are able to start breeding a year after hatching.
Some birds have an orange sheen on their underbellies. This is a normal occurrence for Neophemas, which can also be observed on Turquoisines in the wild.

Sizes and weights
Length: 20cm (8in).
Weights: cock 37-44g, hen 38g.
Ring size: 4mm.

Habitat and habits
Turquoisines have a preference for areas where woods border on open land. These are found on the slopes of the Great Dividing Range, in sheltered valleys, along watercourses, and round grasslands.
They are common within their range, and are found in pairs or small flocks of up to thirty birds. They spend most of the day on the ground foraging for grass seeds; it seems that in the wild they only drink once a day, just before first light.

Diet
They prefer small seeds, particularly those of grasses and herb-like plants on or close to the ground. They also eat green food and some insects and larvae.

71. Turquoisine Grass Parakeet; this splendid orange-bellied form was developed by selectively breeding birds with a lot of orange

72. Turquoisine Grass Parakeet; Yellow or Dilute

Nest-site

They choose a nest-site in a hollow branch or trunk, usually no more than one metre above ground.

In the aviary it is no problem if the box is placed a little higher, as for other Neophemas a box measuring 30 x 15 x 15cm (12 x 6 x 6in) with a 5cm (2in) entrance hole can be used. Of course it does not matter if the box is a couple of centimetres larger or smaller.

Breeding process

Turquoisines can be bred in colonies as long as the aviary is large enough, and preferably planted with bushes. However, care must be taken, as the cocks sometimes develop aggressive behaviour towards each other or to their own sons. Ultimately it is, therefore, often better to have one pair to an aviary, and a length of three metres (10ft) is then sufficient. The hen incubates the four to seven eggs for about eighteen days, and the chicks then fledge a good four weeks later. The cock feeds the hen both inside and outside the box. He will probably start taking interest in the chicks once they are fourteen days old. Some hens add a few blades of grass to the nest using the feathers on their rumps.

If the cock starts chasing his sons around it is better to remove them. If the young birds are not yet independent (normally three weeks after hatching), the cock should be temporarily removed.

The first clutch is often followed by a second, and sometimes even by a third. The fledglings are very nervous and easily startled at first.

An Australian birdkeeper had six pairs in an aviary measuring nine by four metres (30 x 13ft). He found that the young birds had to be removed as soon as they were independent, otherwise the other pairs started fighting with them.

A lady birdkeeper in England had a number of pairs in cages measuring 120 x 60 x 90cm (48 x 24 x 36in); not one of them showed any signs of nesting. When she put the birds outside they all produced chicks.

General remarks

At first sight it is difficult to tell Turquoisine and Splendid hens apart. However, the blue on the wings of Turquoisine hens is darker and the lores, the area between beak and eye, is white; the lores of Splendid hens is blue.

The Turquoisine is the most aggressive of the Neophemas; this can reveal itself particularly during the breeding season.

Breeding presents no real problems; every birdkeeper should be able to achieve success. The breeding stock shows quite a variation of colours; some males are yellower than others, others have greenish bellies, and the amount of orange can vary greatly.

Mutations

The Turquoisine is one of the parakeets of which more and more mutations are gradually appearing. The Yellow-Pied, Olive Green, Yellow and Fallow can be mentioned; but there are also reports of even Blue, Opaline and Lutino mutations. The Orange-bellied Turquoisine should be mentioned separately as it is not a true mutation. Most of these are still rare; the best-known are the Yellow and the Orange-bellied.

The Yellow-Pied has the strange characteristic that the shoulder patch of the cock is not

215

73. Turquoisine Grass parakeet; this Yellow Orange-bellied Turquoisine is the result of Yellow x Orange-bellied

always present, whereas the hen often shows signs of one. This Pied inherits sex-linked recessive.

Little is known about the Olive Green. It was bred some years ago in Denmark, but since then nothing has been heard about this mutation.

The Yellow Turquoisine is becoming more common. However, the name of this mutation is not strictly correct as it is a Dilute bird. However, the now widely accepted name 'Yellow' will be difficult to change. A close inspection of this bird's colour reveals that it is not pure yellow, but more of a pale yellowish-green. All the same it is still a splendid mutation which, due to its autosomal recessive mode of inheritence, produces both split cocks and hens.

The Fallow is a rather faded looking bird with red eyes; the normal green becomes a more greyish-green. It inherits autosomal recessive.

A true Blue Turquoisine has not yet been bred, but the first Dilute Blue birds have appeared, the fronts of which are cream coloured and the backs sea green. These inherit autosomal recessive.

The Opaline has been reported from Germany; its mantle, head and back are a deeper yellow than the normal bird.

The first mention of a Lutino is also from Germany. In Lutinos all the blue colouring becomes white. It could be some years before more is seen of this mutation.

The Orange-bellied Turquoisine is a result of the selective formation of breeding pairs. Birds with orange on their bellies also occur in the wild, and some of these are of course also found in collections. It appears that by constantly pairing the birds with most orange, the depth and extent of the colour increases until a splendid Orange-bellied Turquoisine develops which has orange extending as far as the beak. By pairing these birds with Yellow mutations, Yellow Orange-bellied Turquoisines have been reared.

There are aviculturists that couple another theory to the appearance of the Orange-bellied Turquoisine. According to the Gloger's Law the geographical subspecies from a wet area form more melanine than the subspecies from a drier area, in other words: the wetter the area, the oranger the bird, and the drier the area, the yellower. This means that the Turquoisines in the wetter western Europe should develop more orange in their plumage, and that this phenomemon should then also occur in the other Neophemas.

74. *Splendid Parakeet; the cock is much more colourful than the hen. The red should be broad with a sharp edge*

218

SPLENDID PARAKEET - *Neophema splendida*

Subspecies
None.

Origin of name
Neophema: new sound.
Splendida: splendid.
Dutch: splendid parkiet.
German: Glanzsittich.

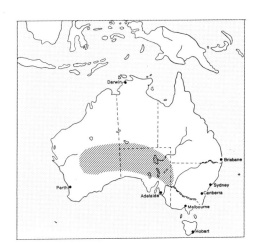

Parents and young
There can be no confusing the cocks and
the hens. The splendid blue head and red
breast of the cock are characteristics
which the hen does not possess.
The amount of red present can vary considerably from cock to cock, and you should pay
attention to this when purchasing. The patch should be as broad as possible and the
borderline with the yellow belly should be as sharply defined as possible. There are
already far too many birds with an undersized red breast.
Young birds look very similar to the hen. Males can already have a little more blue on
their heads, but many have none at all. Once a few months have past the first red feathers
start to come through. Within a year they have developed their adult plumage, but after
this they often become more beautiful still.
They should not be given the opportunity to breed before they are a year old.

Sizes and weights
Length: 20cm (8in).
Weights: cock 40-44g, hen 36-37g.
Ring size: 4mm.

Habitat and habits
The Splendid Parakeet is a bird of the arid desert-like interior of Australia. It is here that,
particularly after the scanty rainfall, the grasses and herbs grow on which it feeds.
Eucalyptus and acacia bushes can also be found here.
During the breeding season the Splendids divide up into pairs, outside it they form small
flocks of ten to twenty birds. During the day, due to the heat particularly in the mornings
and evenings, they forage on the ground or in low bushes for seeds. They roam about in
search of the seeding plants which have grown where rain happens to have fallen. As the
rainfall is impossible to predict, the Splendid Parakeets lead a nomadic existence and
sometimes will not return to places where they have been observed for many years. This,
coupled with the fact that they live in an area which few people visit, has led to the idea
that it is a rare species.

75. *Splendid Parakeet; this Blue cock is generally known as the White-breasted Blue.As it is a pure Blue mutation, the colours red and yellow have disappeared*

76. *Splendid Parakeet; a Silver hen and a Cinnamon cock*

220

However, many observers in Australia are of the opinion that the situation is not serious, and that there are more birds flying about in the wild than was always thought.

Diet
Splendids live mainly on the seeds of grasses and herb-like plants growing on or close to the ground. They have a preference for the seeds of spinifex, a tough grass-like plant which is widespread in the Australian interior. Of course they do not say no to the occasional insect.
They are able to go without water for quite long periods, partly because they are able to extract water from the seeds. They have been observed within their distribution range in places where surface water did not appear to be available within many hundreds of kilometres.

Nest-site
This does not differ from other Neophemas. The nest is virtually always made in a hollow trunk or branch. A number of nests are sometimes found close together. In the wild Splendids only breed when and where sufficient rain has fallen, so that there is enough food available to rear the young.
In the aviary a box measuring 30 x 15 x 15cm (12 x 6 x 6in) with a 5cm (2.5in) diameter entrance hole can be supplied.

Breeding process
Like the Turquoisines Splendids often rear two, or even three, clutches a year. They are generally speaking easy breeders, and it is sometimes said that so much success has been achieved with them that there are more in collections than in the wild.
A clutch consists of four to ten eggs, which are incubated by the hen for about eighteen days. In many nests blades of grass are found which have been brought in by the hen by means of her rump feathers. The cock feeds the hen both inside and outside the box. Once the chicks are about ten days old he assists her with the feeding. The chicks fledge after a good four weeks; after leaving the box they are at first very nervous.
Some cocks are aggressive towards their newly-fledged sons, whereas others show no sign of this. It depends, therefore, on each separate situation whether you, as keeper, should take action.

General remarks
In the description of the Turquoisine is mentioned how to tell the difference between the two hens. It is very important that this is done as nobody has any use for unintentional crosses.
At one time the Splendid Parakeet, as a bird from the hot dry Australian interior, was very susceptible to our chilly damp climate and many birds died. However, as this species has now been bred here for many generations, this is no longer a problem. As is the case for all Neophemas, a certain amount of vegetation can be grown in the aviary, as on the whole they leave this alone.
A three metre (10ft) long flight is sufficient for this species. This parakeet is suitable for

every birdkeeper, from the complete beginner to the experienced old hand. For many people the various mutations present an extra dimension.

Mutations

The Splendid mutations we come across are the Yellow-Pied, Dilute Blue, Blue, Cinnamon, Isabel, Fallow and Red-bellied. There are also rumours about Dark Green and Mauve forms.

In the Pied form a number of green feathers is replaced by yellow ones, and a number of blue by white ones; in both cases this is due to the disappearance of the colour blue. The Pied Splendid is a dominant mutation. When the chicks hatch they are not pied; this appears during the first moult.

The Dilute Blue and Blue forms comprise of the Blue series, in which the yellow gradually retreats and blue comes more and more to the fore. The Blue form is often called the White-breasted Blue; however, this only leads to confusion as this is in fact a pure blue mutation. The colours yellow and red disappear in this form, and thus the breast of the cock becomes white. A certain amount of (paler) red is therefore visible on the first two of the series. All three inherit autosomal recessive.

The Cinnamon and the Isabel look rather similar. The back of the Cinnamon can be described as yellowish-moss green, whereas that of the Isabel is slightly lighter than the normal green. The flight feathers show the clearest difference; the Cinnamon's are beige, and the Isabel's a brownish-grey. Furthermore the blue of the Cinnamon is somewhat brighter. Both inherit sex-linked recessive.

The Fallow can be described as a faded version of the normal bird with dark red eyes. The colours are rather dull. The mode of inheritance is autosomal recessive.

The Dark Green is a darker version of the normal bird, and is therefore in the green series and has dark factor one. The Mauve belongs in the Blue series and has dark factor two.

The same applies to the Red-bellied Splendid as to the Orange-bellied Turquoisine; it has been developed by the selective breeding of birds with a tendency to red or orange. The colour of the belly is a shade lighter than that of the breast.

As with all mutations all sorts of colourings can be developed by pairing new combinations. Examples are the Silver Splendid (from the combination Cinnamon x Blue) and the Sky-Blue Splendid (from the combination Isabel x Blue).

Genus *Lathamus*

The genus *Lathamus* comprises only one species; the Swift Parakeet. Its characteristics and habits differ somewhat from the birds dealt with so far; it can in fact be regarded as an intermediate form between the Parakeets and the Lories. This manifests itself in the bird's behaviour, its diet and in the form of the tongue.

Swift Parakeets clamber about in trees like Lories, seldom come down to the ground, and find their food in blooming eucalyptuses and other nectar-producing trees and bushes. Their tongues are more or less shaped for the eating of nectar and other parts of the blossom, although they do not possess the fully developed brush-like tongue of the Lories.

genus	species	subspecies	
Lathamus	*discolor*	-	Swift Parakeet

77. Swift Parakeet; the cock (right) is often slightly more brightly and extensively coloured

SWIFT PARAKEET - *Lathamus discolor*

Subspecies
None.

Origin of name
Lathamus: after Dr John Latham (1740-
1837), the most famous British ornithol-
ogist from the eighteenth century.
Discolor: varied, pied, many-coloured.
Dutch: swiftparkiet.
German: Schwalbensittich.

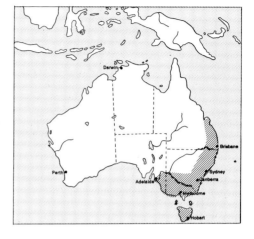

Parents and young
Despite claims to the contrary, the presence or absence of a wing stripe is not
any proof as to the sex of a Swift Parakeet. The difference is by no means always easy to
see. The cock is often more brightly coloured and this is most noticeable by a deeper
green on the body, a deeper and more extensive red on the head and also under the beak,
a deeper yellow beside the beak, and deeper red under tail coverts. The cocks are also said
to have a louder call.
Further, it may be that the cock has orangeish-yellow irises whereas the hen's tend to
brownish-yellow. Finally, the cock is sometimes slightly larger.
Immature birds are much duller than their parents. They develop their full plumage within
about nine months, but this continues to become more beautiful as the birds get older,
particularly the mask. These parakeets are sexually mature within a year of hatching.

Sizes and weights
Length: 25cm (10in).
Weights: 50-74g.
Ring size: 5mm.

Habitat and habits
Swift Parakeets breed only on Tasmania and its surrounding islands. In the autumn they go
to Australia to spend the winter, where they do not inhabit fixed territories but roam
throughout the range. As they are dependent on trees for their food, they can be found
anywhere where there is woodland: on virtually the whole of Tasmania and in southeast
Australia. They prefer dry open deciduous woods.
Swift Parakeets roam about in small noisy groups; their flight resembles that of the Swift,
hence the name. They sometimes form large flocks.
They usually feed on the outside branches of blooming eucalyptus trees. They are typical
tree birds and only come down to the ground in order to drink. Their diet and behaviour
are very similar to the Lories'.

Diet

This species is an intermediate form between the parakeets and the lories. They are found in virtually all the blooming trees and bushes where they extract the nectar from the blossom. This forms the main ingredient of their diet, which also includes many species of insects and larvae, berries and other fruits, seeds, and green food.

Many birdkeepers do not take sufficient account of this, and Swift Parakeets in collections often have to make do with the same menu as other Australian Parakeets, whereas they really should be receiving extra fruit, egg food, lori feed and/or honey.

Nest-site

In the wild they have a preference for holes in gum trees, from just above ground level up to over twenty metres (66ft) high. Sometimes a number of nest is found in one tree.

In aviaries Swift Parakeets will breed in a 35cm (14in) tall box with a floor measuring 18 x 18cm (7 x 7in). The diameter of the entrance hole should be 5.5cm (2.25in).

Breeding process

With the onset of the breeding season the hen selects a suitable nest-site. After some time she lays three to five eggs, and then incubates them for about nineteen days. During this period she is almost entirely dependent on the cock for her food. He occasionally calls her from the nest for feeding. In the wild she seldom returns directly to the nest; she usually flies to a nearby branch and then climbs the rest of the way to the entrance hole. Some branches should, therefore, be arranged around the nest-box in the aviary. The chicks make their first appearance outside the box after about five weeks. Up to this time the hen usually spends the night in the box with them.

The first clutch is sometimes followed by a second, especially if the parents are older.

Swift Parakeets are not aggressive, and breeding in colonies is therefore possible. However, caution is called for, as they are so inquisitive that they may disturb each others nests. If you wish to try this, see to it that there are more nest-boxes than pairs, and that there are no 'single' birds flying around.

General remarks

An aviary three metres (10ft) long is sufficient for these birds. They are active virtually the whole day and scramble and climb about continually. It is therefore a good idea to supply lots of thin branches. Blooming branches are even better, as then the birds will be able to eat the blossoms. As these birds are not destructive, it is possible to plant vegetation in the aviary. Choose species that will bloom.

Swift Parakeets are hardy birds which are not troubled by our low winter temperatures. They can become quite tame, and are very keen on bathing.

Mutations

A Yellow Swift Parakeet has been bred. However, it is not pure yellow in colour, but yellowish-green. The plumage is dilute coloured and the head a dull blue. The form of inheritance is reported as being sex-linked recessive.

Genus *Melopsittacus*

This genus comprises one species. This single member is known throughout the world and has risen victoriously to the position of being one of the most successful pets and aviary birds. On mentioning parakeets it is this bird which first springs to mind. The Budgerigar is a small parrotlike with a pointed tail. It is probably an intermediate form between the genuses *Neophema* and *Pezoporus* (Ground Parakeet; not found in collections), and it has the slightly wavy pattern on the plumage in common with the latter.

genus	species	subspecies	
Melopsittacus	*undulatus*	-	Budgerigar

78. Budgerigar; the Normal form and a Blue mutation

BUDGERIGAR - *Melopsittacus undulatus*

Subspecies
None.

Origin of name
Melopsittacus: singing parakeet.
Undulatus: wavy.
Dutch: grasparkiet.
German: Wellensittich.

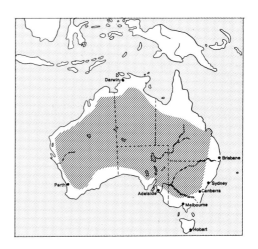

Parents and young
Cocks and hens have the same plumage; the only difference is to be found in the colour of the nostrils at the top of the beak: the cocks' are blue and the hens' are flesh-coloured. Young birds are duller than their parents and the dark spots on the throat are less distinct. They develop their full plumage in three to six months. It is inadvisable to let them breed before they are nine months old. However, they will probably start earlier if they find a suitable partner and there is a nest-box available.

Sizes and weights
Length: 18cm (7in).
Weights: cock 26-29g, hen 27-29g.
Ring size: 4mm.
The length and the weights here are applicable to the wild birds in Australia. As a result of selective breeding the figures for exhibition birds may well be slightly higher.

Habitat and habits
The Budgerigar is found in the whole of Australia, with the exception of the coastal areas. It chiefly inhabits areas with scattered trees, the arid interior, and semi-arid and damp regions; it is also found in eucalyptus bushes and on agricultural land. It is common in most of these areas, although the numbers can vary enormously. It is probably the most numerous parrotlike in the continent. There are reports of sightings of huge flocks containing as many as 20,000 birds. In one eucalyptus branches with a diameter of four centimtres broke.
Such occurrences usually take place only in the interior near water. Although it has been shown that Budgerigars can go without water for long periods, in the wild they are not often found far from it; during droughts they abandon the areas in which the water supply has dried up. ·
These little parakeets are most active in the early morning and towards dusk, when they search for water and food. The rest of the day they can be found in sheltered spots where

229

they spend the hottest hours sitting immobile and quiet. They lead a nomadic existence, as they often follow the rains.

Diet

Budgerigars live almost entirely on the seeds of grasses, among others Spinifex, and other plants which grow on or close to the ground. Birdkeepers often supply larger amounts of smaller seeds than for bigger Australian parakeets.

Nest-site

When wild Budgerigars get the urge to nest, and particularly after rain, they make use of every available cavity. They prefer holes in trees, but nests are even found on the ground. Breeding in colonies is common in the wild and sometimes a number of nests is found in one branch.

In aviaries and in breeding cages small nest-boxes 15cm (6in) tall and with a floor measuring 12 x 20cm (5 x 8in) are widely used; an entrance hole with a diameter of 5cm (2in) is sufficient.

Breeding process

In Australia Budgerigars nest throughout the year, depending on when the rain falls. They often breed twice a year, though not in the same place. Birds which inhabit areas in which water is virtually always available, rear their young at more fixed times. It seems that in the wild young cocks are able to produce sperm at an age of only sixty days.

The hen lays an egg every other day; once the clutch is complete she incubates the four to eight eggs alone. She is fed by the cock mainly in the early morning and late afternoon. Incubation takes eighteen days. If the young grow well, they leave the box after about thirty-two days. A few weeks later they are independent.

General remarks

There are various ways of keeping Budgerigars. The birdkeeper who just wants a few birds can release a group into an aviary, hang up a couple of nest-boxes and let them get on with it. However, he should not be too particular about the quality of the young he rears. In practice this applies to every situation in which a number of birds of this species are housed together.

If Budgerigars are being reared for exhibitions it is absolutely essential that they are housed in pairs, and that the birds which are to be placed together undergo careful selection. A visit to any exhibition will show that such birds have a different shape and colour than the average pet Budgie. The difference in the size and appearance of these birds is a result of very selective breeding. If Budgerigars are to be kept to this end, the simplest method is to breed them in cages. In that case a cage for one pair should be at least 80cm (32in) long, 50cm (20in) high and 40cm (16in) deep.

Mutations

The first Budgerigars to reach western Europe arrived in England in about 1840. The first mutation, and it was the Yellow, appeared thirty-five years later in Belgium. The first Blue mutation was developed in the Netherlands in 1881, and it was from a pair of these mutations that the first Albinos were accidently bred in 1920. After that mutations appeared regularly. At the present time for the purpose of exhibitions there are at least fourteen groups in which they can be judged: Normal Green, Normal Blue, Opaline Green, Opaline Blue, Cinnamon Green, Cinnamon Blue, combination of Opaline and Cinnamon, Pied, Crested, etc. And then there are about another seventy-five classes distinguishable within these groups!

It goes far beyond the scope of this book to deal fully with all the various mutations; within aviculture Budgerigars form a branch of their own which exists independent of the rest. I will limit myself here to the two latest mutations developed in the Netherlands of which only a few birds have been reared. This concerns the Silver-coloured (white in appearance) which has retained the black pattern on wings, back and head, and the Golden-coloured.

The first is the result of a cross between a Violet White-winged cock and an Opaline-Cobalt hen. This was probably the result of a deviation, as the breeder can still not offer any explanation, even though he has full knowledge of the characteristics of the parents. They would have been expected to produce Mauve, Violet, Cobalt, Blue, and Violet-Cinnamon young. The aberrant bird has a completely white breast and belly, whereas, as already mentioned, the black pattern on the head, back and wings has remained. Examination of the feather structure has shown that this bird is not a White but a Silver mutation.

As this male bird was the offspring of parents from the Blue series, it was first paired with a Blue mutation; the young produced retained a blue sheen on their rumps.

The Silver cock was then paired with a Grey hen. As some of the offspring were Silver, this is probably a dominant mutation.

At a later stage a Silver hen was paired with a Grey-Green cock. It appeared that this combination produces almost Golden-coloured Budgerigars! However, as the rump of these birds has a pale green sheen the breeder thinks it would probably be better to arrange a pairing with a pure Light Green, as this could result in a better colour on the rump and a brighter body colour. Both mutations are shown in the photograph.

Only time will tell if these mutations will be the beginning of new developments within the hobby of Budgerigar keeping.

79. Budgerigar; the latest mutations; Silver-black and Golden-coloured

Literature

J.M. Forshaw: *'Parrots of the World'*. Melbourne 1989.
J.M. Forshaw: *'Australian Parrots'*. Melbourne 1981.
H.D. Groen: *'Australische parkieten'*. Haren 1967.
I. Harman: *'Australian Parrots'*. London 1981.
J.P. Holsheimer: *'Voeding van vogels'*. Zutphen 1980.
J.P. Holsheimer: *'Ziekten van vogels'*. Zutphen 1979.
J.P. Holsheimer: *'Ziekten van kooi- en volièrevogels'*. Zutphen 1983.
B.R. Hutchins & R.H. Lovell: *'Australian parrots, a field and aviary study'*. Melbourne 1985.
K. Immelmann: *'De Australische platstaartparkieten'*. Hoboken.
G.Th.F. Kaal: *'Gezondheidszorg bij papegaaien, parkieten, kakatoes, agaporniden, lori's'*. Arnhem 1982.
H. Köster: *'Die Grassittiche'*. Köln 1983.
A.H. Lendon: *'Australian parrots in field and aviary'*. Melbourne 1976.
R. Low: *'Parrots, their care and breeding'*. Poole 1980.
Royal Australasian Ornithologists Union: *'The Atlas of Australian Birds'*. Melbourne 1984.
G.A. Smith: *'Lovebirds and Related Parrots'*. London 1979.
G.A. Smith: *'Encyclopedia of Cockatiels'*. 1978.
H.P.M. Zomer: *'Neophema's en hun kleurmutaties'*. Arnhem 1987.

Magazines:

Australian Aviculture
AZ-Nachrichten
Cage & Aviary Birds
Die Gefiederte Welt
Die Voliere
Gefiederter Freund
Onze Parkieten
Onze Vogels
Parkieten Sociëteit
Parrot Society